MW01282342

Entertainment Directory

PARIS

SHOPPING GUIDE 2019

RECOMMENDED STORES FOR VISITORS

The Most Positively Reviewed and Recommended Stores in the City

ECP
Editorial

PARIS SHOPPING GUIDE 2019
Best Rated Stores in the City

© Anne B. Allan, 2019
© E.G.P. Editorial, 2019

ISBN-13: 978-1721825837
ISBN-10: 1721825835

Copyright © 2019
All rights reserved.

PARIS SHOPPING GUIDE 2019

Best Rated Stores in the City

*This directory is dedicated to the Business Owners and Managers
who provide the experience that the locals and tourists enjoy.
Thanks you very much for all that you do and thank for being the "People Choice".*

*Thanks to everyone that posts their reviews online and
the amazing reviews sites that make our life easier.*

*The places listed in this book are the most positively reviewed
and recommended by locals and travelers from around the world.*

*Thank you for your time and enjoy the directory that is
designed with locals and tourist in mind!*

TOP 500
SHOPPING SPOTS
The Most Recommended
(from #1 to #500)

#1
Galeries Lafayette Haussmann
Category: Department Stores
Average Price: Expensive
Area: 9ème, Saint-Lazare/Grands Magasins
Address: 40 Boulevard Haussmann
75009 Paris France
Phone: 01 42 82 34 56

#2
Bercy Village
Category: Shopping Centers
Average Price: Modest
Area: Bercy, 12ème
Address: 28 Rue François Truffaut
75012 Paris France
Phone: 08 25 16 60 75

#3
Beaugrenelle
Category: Shopping Centers
Average Price: Modest
Area: Auteuil, 15ème
Address: 12 Rue Linois
75015 Paris France
Phone: 01 53 95 24 00

#4
Merci
Category: Department Stores
Average Price: Expensive
Area: Marais Nord, 3ème, Marais
Address: 111 Boulevard Beaumarchais
75003 Paris France
Phone: 01 42 77 00 33

#5
Le Passage Jouffroy
Category: Shopping Centers
Average Price: Modest
Area: Richelieu-Drouot, 9ème
Address: Passage Jouffroy
75009 Paris France
Phone: 01 48 24 03 83

#6
Carrousel Du Louvre
Category: Shopping Centers
Average Price: Expensive
Area: 1er, Palais Royal/Musée Du Louvre
Address: 99 Rue De Rivoli
75001 Paris France
Phone: 01 43 16 47 10

#7
La Piscine
Category: Men's Clothing, Women's Clothing
Average Price: Modest
Area: Saint-Michel/Odéon
Address: 19-21 Rue De l'Ancienne
Comédie 75006 Paris France
Phone: 01 44 07 01 38

#8
Le Bon Marché
Category: Department Stores
Average Price: Expensive
Area: 7ème
Address: 24 Rue De Sèvres
75007 Paris France
Phone: 01 44 39 80 00

#9
Paulie And Me...
Category: Jewelry, Accessories,
Women's Clothing
Average Price: Modest
Area: Châtelet/Les Halles, 1er
Address: 68 Rue Jean Jacques
Rousseau 75001 Paris France
Phone: 06 85 94 04 34

#10
Hema
Category: Department Stores
Average Price: Inexpensive
Area: Bastille
Address: 86 Rue Du Faubourg
Saint-Antoine 75012 Paris France
Phone: 01 44 68 02 70

#11
Monoprix
Category: Department Stores
Average Price: Modest
Area: Bastille, Marais, 4ème
Address: 71 Rue Saint-Antoine
75004 Paris France
Phone: 01 42 74 13 73

#12
Les Grands Voisins
Category: Shopping Centers
Average Price: Modest
Area: Denfert-Rochereau, 14ème
Address: 82 Avenue Denfert-Rochereau
75014 Paris France
Phone: 07 83 76 21 00

#13
Vintage Désir
Category: Used, Vintage & Consignment
Average Price: Inexpensive
Area: Marais, 4ème
Address: 32 Rue Des Rosiers
75004 Paris France
Phone: 01 40 27 04 98

#14
La Piscine
Category: Men's Clothing, Women's Clothing
Average Price: Modest
Area: Montmartre, 18ème
Address: 29 Bis Rue Des Abbesses
75018 Paris France
Phone: 01 42 55 94 45

#15
Hema
Category: Department Stores
Average Price: Inexpensive
Area: Châtelet/Les Halles, 1er
Address: 120 Rue Rambuteau
75001 Paris France
Phone: 01 45 08 09 27

#16
Centre Commercial
Category: Fashion
Average Price: Expensive
Area: Canal St Martin/Gare De l'Est, 10ème
Address: 2 Rue De Marseille
75010 Paris France
Phone: 01 42 02 26 68

#17
Isabel Marant Diffusion
Category: Women's Clothing
Average Price: Expensive
Area: Marais Nord, 3ème
Address: 47 Rue Saintonge
75003 Paris France
Phone: 01 42 78 19 24

#18
Louis Vuitton
Category: Leather Goods,
Luggage, Accessories
Average Price: Expensive
Area: Place Vendôme, 1er
Address: 23 Place Vendôme
75001 Paris France
Phone: 01 81 69 27 50

#19
So We Are
Category: Accessories, Women's Clothing
Average Price: Expensive
Area: Ledru-Rollin, 11ème
Address: 40 Rue De Charonne
75011 Paris France
Phone: 09 82 37 63 91

#20
COS
Category: Men's Clothing, Women's Clothing
Average Price: Modest
Area: Marais, 4ème
Address: 4 Rue Des Rosiers
75004 Paris France
Phone: 01 70 70 33 90

#21
Matières À Réflexion
Category: Accessories, Leather Goods,
Women's Clothing
Average Price: Modest
Area: Marais Nord, 3ème, Marais
Address: 19 Rue De Poitou
75003 Paris France
Phone: 01 42 72 16 31

#22
Monoprix
Category: Department Stores
Average Price: Modest
Area: 9ème, Richelieu-Drouot
Address: 12 Rue Châteaudun
75009 Paris France
Phone: 01 44 91 81 80

#23
Lola Jones
Category: Women's Clothing
Average Price: Modest
Area: 15ème, Vaugirard/Grenelle
Address: 115 Rue Du Théâtre
75015 Paris France
Phone: 01 40 59 80 40

#24
Monoprix
Category: Department Stores
Average Price: Modest
Area: Glacière/Cité Universitaire, 13ème
Address: 42 Rue Daviel
75013 Paris France
Phone: 01 45 80 97 01

#25
L'Eclaireur
Category: Men's Clothing,
Women's Clothing, Accessories
Average Price: Exclusive
Area: Marais, 3ème
Address: 40 Rue De Sévigné
75003 Paris France
Phone: 01 48 87 10 22

#26
Acne
Category: Men's Clothing, Women's Clothing,
Children's Clothing
Average Price: Expensive
Area: Marais Nord, 3ème, Marais
Address: 3 Rue Froissart
75003 Paris France
Phone: 01 49 96 96 91

#27
Monoprix
Category: Grocery, Department Stores
Average Price: Expensive
Area: La Villette, 19ème
Address: 13 Ave Secrétan
75019 Paris France
Phone: 01 42 03 15 03

#28
Anoki
Category: Accessories
Average Price: Modest
Area: Montmartre, 18ème
Address: 3 Rue Tardieu
75018 Paris France
Phone: 01 71 37 95 18

#29
Isabel Marant
Category: Women's Clothing
Average Price: Expensive
Area: Bastille, 11ème
Address: 16 Rue Charonne
75011 Paris France
Phone: 01 49 29 71 55

#30
Vintage Désir
Category: Used, Vintage & Consignment
Average Price: Inexpensive
Area: Montmartre, 18ème
Address: 28 Rue Yvonne Le Tac
75018 Paris France
Phone: 01 42 57 96 56

#31
Monoprix
Category: Department Stores
Average Price: Modest
Area: Vaugirard/Grenelle, 15ème
Address: 2 Rue Du Commerce
75015 Paris France
Phone: 01 45 79 94 86

#33
Vintage Madeleine
Category: Used, Vintage & Consignment
Average Price: Modest
Area: Concorde/Madeleine, 8ème
Address: 31 Rue Anjou
75008 Paris France
Phone: 01 40 07 52 96

#32
Antoine Et Lili
Category: Accessories, Women's Clothing
Average Price: Modest
Area: Canal St Martin/Gare De l'Est, 10ème
Address: 95 Quai Valmy
75010 Paris France
Phone: 01 40 37 58 14

#34
Chanel
Category: Women's Clothing,
Accessories, Perfume
Average Price: Exclusive
Area: Avenue Montaigne/Faubourg St-
Honoré, 8ème
Address: 42 Avenue Montaigne
75008 Paris France
Phone: 01 40 70 82 00

#35
La Galerie - Masséna
Category: Shopping Centers
Average Price: Exclusive
Area: Place d'Italie, 13ème
Address: 98 Boulevard Masséna
75013 Paris France
Phone: 01 45 84 08 40

#36
Louis Vuitton
Category: Luggage, Leather Goods,
Women's Clothing
Average Price: Exclusive
Area: Champs-Elysées, 8ème
Address: 101 Ave Des Champs-Elysées
75008 Paris France
Phone: 01 53 57 52 00

#37
Babel Concept Store
Category: Concept Shops, Home Decor
Average Price: Modest
Area: Canal St Martin/Gare De l'Est, 10ème
Address: 55 Quai De Valmy
75010 Paris France
Phone: 01 42 40 10 95

#38
Diwali
Category: Accessories, Jewelry
Average Price: Modest
Area: Saint-Michel/Odéon, 6ème
Address: 40 Rue Saint-André Des Arts
75006 Paris France
Phone: 01 43 29 10 09

#39
Supermarché De La Madone
Category: Department Stores
Average Price: Modest
Area: 18ème
Address: 5 Rue Madone
75018 Paris France
Phone: 01 46 07 72 59

#40
Paul & Lou
Category: Women's Clothing, Men's Clothing
Average Price: Modest
Area: 15ème, Vaugirard/Grenelle
Address: 115 Rue Du Théâtre
75015 Paris France
Phone: 01 45 77 80 76

#41
Sneakersnstuff
Category: Accessories, Shoe Stores,
Women's Clothing
Average Price: Expensive
Area: Etienne Marcel/Montorgueil, Grands
Boulevards/Sentier, 2ème
Address: 95 Rue Réaumur
75002 Paris France
Phone: 01 44 82 95 41

#42
Chanel
Category: Cosmetics & Beauty Supply,
Accessories, Women's Clothing
Average Price: Exclusive
Area: Concorde/Madeleine, 1er
Address: 31 Rue Cambon
75001 Paris France
Phone: 01 44 50 66 00

#43
Outlet Demarque
Category: Outlet Stores
Average Price: Expensive
Area: Saint-Lazare/Grands Magasins, 8ème
Address: 3 Rue Du Havre
75008 Paris France
Phone: 01 58 34 96 76

#44
Tati
Category: Fashion
Average Price: Inexpensive
Area: Barbès/Goutte d'Or, 18ème
Address: 18 Bd Rochechouart
75018 Paris France
Phone: 01 55 29 50 00

#45
Fina Collections
Category: Men's Clothing, Women's Clothing,
Children's Clothing
Average Price: Modest
Area: Strasbourg-St Denis/Bonne
Nouvelle, 10ème
Address: 1 Rue Paradis
75010 Paris France
Phone: 01 40 22 02 71

#46
Monoprix
Category: Department Stores
Average Price: Modest
Area: 12ème, Bercy
Address: 237 Ave Daumesnil
75012 Paris France
Phone: 01 43 43 40 03

#47
Hema
Category: Department Stores
Average Price: Inexpensive
Area: Richelieu-Drouot, 9ème
Address: 2 Bd Haussmann
75009 Paris France
Phone: 01 42 46 36 27

#48
Monoprix
Category: Department Stores
Average Price: Expensive
Area: Auteuil, 16ème
Address: 18 Rue De Passy
75116 Paris France
Phone: 01 45 20 17 52

#49
Topshop
Category: Women's Clothing
Average Price: Modest
Area: Pigalle, 9ème
Address: 40 Bd Haussmann
75009 Paris France
Phone: 01 42 82 34 56

#50
Yves Saint Laurent
Category: Men's Clothing, Women's Clothing
Average Price: Expensive
Area: Concorde/Madeleine, 8ème
Address: 38 Rue Fbg St Honoré
75008 Paris France
Phone: 01 42 65 74 59

#51
Artling
Category: Accessories, Bespoke Clothing
Average Price: Inexpensive
Area: Saint-Germain-Des-Prés, 6ème
Address: 55 Rue Des Saints-Pères
75006 Paris France
Phone: 01 42 22 99 92

#52
Chez Nana
Category: Jewelry
Average Price: Inexpensive
Area: Strasbourg-St Denis/Bonne
Nouvelle, 10ème
Address: 19 Rue d'Hauteville
75010 Paris France
Phone: 01 77 10 11 09

#53
Monoprix
Category: Department Stores
Average Price: Expensive
Area: Nation/Vincennes, 20ème
Address: 20 Bd De Charonne
75020 Paris France
Phone: 01 43 73 17 59

#54
Monoprix
Category: Department Stores
Average Price: Modest
Area: Champs-Elysées, 17ème
Address: 25 Avenue Des Ternes
75017 Paris France
Phone: 01 43 80 43 76

#55
La Piscine
Category: Men's Clothing, Women's Clothing
Average Price: Modest
Area: Pereire/Cardinet/Courcelles, 17ème
Address: 104 Rue De Courcelles
75017 Paris France
Phone: 01 47 63 85 17

#56
Monki
Category: Women's Clothing, Accessories
Average Price: Modest
Area: Saint-Lazare/Grands Magasins, 9ème
Address: 96 Rue De Provence
75009 Paris France
Phone: 01 53 32 85 00

#57
The Shop Around The Corner
Category: Accessories, Shoe Stores,
Women's Clothing
Average Price: Modest
Area: 11ème, Père Lachaise
Address: 137 Rue De Charonne
75011 Paris France
Phone: 01 43 48 39 80

#58
Printemps
Category: Department Stores
Average Price: Expensive
Area: Saint-Lazare/Grands Magasins, 9ème
Address: 64 Boulevard Haussmann
75009 Paris France
Phone: 01 42 82 50 00

#59
Picsouille
Category: Used, Vintage & Consignment
Average Price: Modest
Area: Châtelet/Les Halles, 1er, Palais
Royal/Musée Du Louvre
Address: 3 Rue Perrault
75001 Paris France
Phone: 01 42 60 65 05

#60
Passy Plaza
Category: Department Stores
Average Price: Expensive
Area: Auteuil, 16ème
Address: 53 Rue Passy
75016 Paris France
Phone: 01 44 14 50 40

#61
Les Parisettes
Category: Gift Shops
Average Price: Modest
Area: 15ème, Vaugirard/Grenelle, Auteuil
Address: 10 Rue Gramme
75015 Paris France
Phone: 01 75 43 23 65

#62
Pimkie
Category: Fashion
Average Price: Inexpensive
Area: Saint-Michel/Odéon, 6ème
Address: 25 Boulevard St Michel
75005 Paris France
Phone: 01 44 27 06 02

#63
Nice Piece
Category: Women's Clothing, Men's Clothing
Average Price: Modest
Area: Marais Nord, 3ème
Address: 76 Rue Charlot
75003 Paris France
Phone: 01 42 77 29 76

#64
A La Boule Magique
Category: Arts & Crafts, Jewelry
Average Price: Modest
Area: Oberkampf/Parmentier, 11ème
Address: 98 Rue Oberkampf
75011 Paris France
Phone: 01 43 14 25 75

#65
Mademoiselle Jeanne
Category: Women's Clothing, Accessories
Average Price: Expensive
Area: Ledru-Rollin, 11ème
Address: 55 Rue De La Roquette
75011 Paris France
Phone: 01 43 38 00 70

#66
La Frange À l'Envers
Category: Women's Clothing, Used, Vintage
& Consignment, Shoe Stores
Average Price: Modest
Area: Oberkampf/Parmentier, 11ème
Address: 81 Rue Saint Maur
75011 Paris France
Phone: 06 51 61 56 03

#67
La Halle Saint-Pierre
Category: Art Galleries, Museums
Average Price: Inexpensive
Area: Montmartre, 18ème
Address: 2 Rue Ronsard
75018 Paris France
Phone: 01 42 58 72 89

#68
Kouka
Category: Women's Clothing
Average Price: Inexpensive
Area: Montmartre, 18ème
Address: 32 Bd Rochechouart
75018 Paris France
Phone: 01 42 62 22 58

#69
Uniqlo
Category: Women's Clothing, Men's Clothing,
Children's Clothing
Average Price: Modest
Area: Marais, 4ème
Address: 39 Rue Des Francs
Bourgeois 75004 Paris France
Phone: 01 53 01 87 87

#70
Monoprix
Category: Department Stores
Average Price: Modest
Area: Place De Clichy, 17ème
Address: 43 Avenue Clichy
75017 Paris France
Phone: 01 42 93 22 04

#71
APC Surplus
Category: Men's Clothing,
Women's Clothing, Accessories
Average Price: Expensive
Area: Montmartre, 18ème
Address: 20 Rue André Del Sarte
75018 Paris France
Phone: 01 42 62 10 88

#72
Eunhwa
Category: Women's Clothing
Average Price: Modest
Area: 5ème, Sorbonne/Panthéon
Address: 19 Rue Claude Bernard
75005 Paris France
Phone: 01 42 50 69 20

#73
Joy
Category: Jewelry, Accessories,
Women's Clothing
Average Price: Expensive
Area: Marais, 4ème
Address: 38 Rue Du Roi De Sicile
75004 Paris France
Phone: 09 52 58 38 38

#74
Chez Paulette
Category: Women's Clothing, Used, Vintage
& Consignment, Accessories
Average Price: Inexpensive
Area: Colonel Fabien/Goncourt, 10ème
Address: 32 Rue Bichat
75010 Paris France
Phone: 01 42 08 92 76

#75
Blue Lemon
Category: Accessories
Average Price: Modest
Area: Etienne Marcel/Montorgueil, 2ème
Address: 54 Rue Tiquetonne
75002 Paris France
Phone: 01 42 33 34 73

#76
Bù Store
Category: Shopping Centers
Average Price: Modest
Area: 5ème, Jardin Des Plantes/Austerlitz
Address: 45 Rue Jussieu
75005 Paris France
Phone: 01 40 56 33 22

#77
Lina Nueva
Category: Fashion, Shopping Centers
Average Price: Expensive
Area: 16ème
Address: 2 Place Porte Maillot
75017 Paris France
Phone: 09 69 80 11 66

#78
Côte À Côte
Category: Men's Clothing, Women's Clothing
Average Price: Modest
Area: Saint-Michel/Odéon, 5ème
Address: 15 Bd Saint-Michel
75005 Paris France
Phone: 01 46 33 17 53

#79
Tempolino
Category: Antiques, Used,
Vintage & Consignment
Average Price: Inexpensive
Area: 9ème
Address: 5 Rue Gérando
75009 Paris France
Phone: 06 86 73 75 33

#80
Heroines
Category: Accessories, Women's Clothing
Average Price: Modest
Area: Marais, 4ème
Address: 6 Rue Des Rosiers
75004 Paris France
Phone: 01 42 74 09 91

#81
Maison Kitsuné
Category: Men's Clothing, Women's Clothing
Average Price: Expensive
Area: Marais Nord, 11ème
Address: 18 Bd Des Filles Du Calvaire
75011 Paris France
Phone: 01 58 30 12 37

#82
Hermès
Category: Women's Clothing, Men's Clothing
Average Price: Exclusive
Area: Concorde/Madeleine, 8ème
Address: 24 Rue Du Faubourg Saint-Honoré
75008 Paris France
Phone: 01 40 17 46 00

#83
Lili Cabas
Category: Women's Clothing
Average Price: Modest
Area: Strasbourg-St Denis/Bonne Nouvelle,
10ème
Address: 24 Rue Des Petites Ecuries
75010 Paris France
Phone: 09 54 40 00 16

#84
Jade Et Clara
Category: Women's Clothing
Average Price: Modest
Area: Vaugirard/Grenelle, 15ème
Address: 34 Rue Commerce
75015 Paris France
Phone: 01 45 75 21 84

#85
Les Fleurs
Category: Jewelry, Accessories, Gift Shops
Average Price: Expensive
Area: Ledru-Rollin, 11ème
Address: 5 Rue Trousseau
75011 Paris France
Phone: 01 43 55 12 94

#86
Pierre Caron Bijoux
Category: Fashion
Average Price: Modest
Area: Marais, Marais Nord, 4ème
Address: 52 Rue Archives
75004 Paris France
Phone: 09 65 21 73 14

#87
Acne Studio
Category: Women's Clothing,
Men's Clothing, Accessories
Average Price: Exclusive
Area: Palais Royal/Musée Du Louvre, 1er
Address: 124 Galerie Valois
75001 Paris France
Phone: 01 42 60 16 62

#88
Promod
Category: Women's Clothing
Average Price: Inexpensive
Area: Champs-Elysées, 8ème
Address: 86 Ave Champs Elysées
75008 Paris France
Phone: 01 53 53 02 30

#89
Dileme
Category: Fashion
Average Price: Modest
Area: Bastille, Marais, 4ème
Address: 48 Rue St Antoine
75004 Paris France
Phone: 01 44 78 05 28

#90
Thanx God I'm A V.I.P
Category: Used, Vintage & Consignment
Average Price: Expensive
Area: République
Address: 12 Rue De Lancry
75010 Paris France
Phone: 01 42 03 02 09

#91
Oh Lumière
Category: Used, Vintage & Consignment
Average Price: Inexpensive
Area: Oberkampf/Parmentier, 11ème
Address: 21 Avenue République
75011 Paris France
Phone: 01 43 57 51 26

#92
Mamz'Elle Swing
Category: Women's Clothing, Leather Goods
Average Price: Modest
Area: Marais, 4ème
Address: 35 Bis Rue Du Roi De Sicile
75004 Paris France
Phone: 01 48 87 04 06

#93
Le Mutant
Category: Women's Clothing, Accessories
Average Price: Inexpensive
Area: Canal St Martin/Gare De l'Est, 10ème
Address: 65 Rue De Lancry
75010 Paris France
Phone: 01 42 00 51 96

#94
Episode
Category: Used, Vintage & Consignment
Average Price: Modest
Area: Etienne Marcel/Montorgueil, 2ème
Address: 12-16 Rue Tiquetonne
75002 Paris France
Phone: 01 42 61 14 64

#95
Les Fruits Du Temps
Category: Souvenir Shops
Average Price: Modest
Area: Île De La Cité/Île Saint Louis, 4ème
Address: 80 Rue Saint Louis En L'ile
75004 Paris France
Phone: 01 43 25 87 56

#96
Monoprix
Category: Department Stores
Average Price: Modest
Area: 12ème, Bercy
Address: 215 Rue Charenton
75012 Paris France
Phone: 01 44 67 72 66

#97
Weber Metaux
Category: Outlet Stores
Average Price: Modest
Area: Marais Nord, Marais, 3ème
Address: 66 Rue De Turenne
75003 Paris France
Phone: 01 46 72 34 00

#98
BHV
Category: Department Stores
Average Price: Expensive
Area: Beaubourg, 4ème, Marais
Address: 52 Rue De Rivoli
75004 Paris France
Phone: 09 77 40 14 00

#99
Pimkie
Category: Women's Clothing
Average Price: Inexpensive
Area: Vaugirard/Grenelle, 15ème
Address: 8 Rue Du Commerce
75015 Paris France
Phone: 01 45 75 05 27

#100
Par'Ici - Souvenir De Paris
Category: Gift Shops, Souvenir Shops
Average Price: Inexpensive
Area: 5ème, Sorbonne/Panthéon
Address: 52 Rue Mouffetard
75005 Paris France
Phone: 01 43 31 79 85

#101
Le Corner
Category: Women's Clothing, Concept
Shops, Jewelry
Average Price: Modest
Area: Bastille, 11ème
Address: 24 Rue De Lappe
75011 Paris France
Phone: 09 50 13 20 10

#102
Papier Tigre
Category: Concept Shops, Cards &
Stationery, Home Decor
Average Price: Modest
Area: Marais Nord, 3ème, Marais
Address: 5 Rue Des Filles Du Calvaire
75003 Paris France
Phone: 01 48 04 00 21

#103
Désordre Urbain
Category: Women's Clothing,
Jewelry, Home Decor
Average Price: Modest
Area: Batignolles, 17ème
Address: 96 Rue Nollet
75017 Paris France
Phone: 01 44 85 52 27

#104
Paperdolls
Category: Women's Clothing,
Accessories, Shoe Stores
Average Price: Modest
Area: Pigalle, Montmartre, 18ème
Address: 5 Rue Houdon
75018 Paris France
Phone: 01 42 51 29 87

#105
Shindo
Category: Accessories
Average Price: Modest
Area: 2ème, Bourse
Address: 2 Rue d'Aboukir
75002 Paris France
Phone: 01 44 88 27 56

#106
Comptoir Des Cotonniers
Category: Women's Clothing
Average Price: Modest
Area: Bastille, Marais, 4ème
Address: 18 Rue St Antoine
75004 Paris France
Phone: 01 40 27 09 08

#107
Debut
Category: Used, Vintage & Consignment,
Women's Clothing
Average Price: Inexpensive
Area: La Villette, Buttes Chaumont, 19ème
Address: 28 Avenue Laumière
75019 Paris France
Phone: 01 42 02 47 06

#108
La Petite Boutique
Category: Women's Clothing
Average Price: Modest
Area: Saint-Michel/Odéon, 6ème
Address: 52 Rue Saint Andre Des Arts
75006 Paris France
Phone: 01 83 95 86 41

#109
Merry Jean's
Category: Accessories
Average Price: Modest
Area: Beaubourg, 4ème
Address: 81 Rue Saint-Martin
75004 Paris France
Phone: 01 42 71 10 88

#110
Surface To Air
Category: Fashion
Average Price: Expensive
Area: Marais Nord, 3ème, Marais
Address: 108 Rue Vieille Du Temple
75003 Paris France
Phone: 01 44 61 76 27

#111
Monoprix
Category: Department Stores
Average Price: Modest
Area: Arts & Métiers/Rambuteau
Address: 164 Rue Du Temple
75003 Paris France
Phone: 01 48 87 46 60

#112
78isl
Category: Women's Clothing, Leather Goods
Average Price: Modest
Area: Île De La Cité/Île Saint Louis, 4ème
Address: 78 Rue Saint-Louis En L'ile
75004 Paris France
Phone: 01 40 46 06 36

#113
Spree
Category: Concept Shops, Accessories,
Women's Clothing
Average Price: Expensive
Area: Montmartre, 18ème
Address: 16 Rue La Vieuville
75018 Paris France
Phone: 01 42 23 41 40

#114
Vill'Up
Category: Shopping Centers
Average Price: Modest
Area: 19ème, La Villette
Address: 30 Avenue Corentin Cariou
75019 Paris France
Phone: 01 49 70 83 30

#115
Madeleine & Gustave
Category: Home Decor, Concept Shops
Average Price: Modest
Area: République
Address: 19 Rue Yves Toudic
75010 Paris France
Phone: 01 40 38 61 02

#116
Cosmos
Category: Women's Clothing
Average Price: Inexpensive
Area: Saint-Germain-Des-Prés, 6ème
Address: 154 Boulevard Saint Germain
75006 Paris France
Phone: 01 43 26 29 11

#117
Nana
Category: Women's Clothing
Average Price: Modest
Area: Mairie Du 18e/Lamarck, 18ème
Address: 119 Rue Caulaincourt
75018 Paris France
Phone: 01 46 06 60 79

#118
La Cocotte
Category: Concept Shops,
Hobby Shops, Gift Shops
Average Price: Modest
Area: Ledru-Rollin, Nation/Vincennes, 11ème
Address: 5 Rue Paul Bert
75011 Paris France
Phone: 09 54 73 17 77

#119
Céline
Category: Leather Goods, Women's Clothing
Average Price: Modest
Area: Champs-Elysées, 16ème
Address: 3 Ave Victor Hugo
75116 Paris France
Phone: 01 45 01 80 01

#120
Pylones
Category: Home Decor, Jewelry, Gift Shops
Average Price: Modest
Area: Île De La Cité/Île Saint Louis, 4ème
Address: 57 Rue Saint Louis En I'lle
75004 Paris France
Phone: 01 46 34 05 02

#121
My Bootik
Category: Accessories, Women's Clothing
Average Price: Modest
Area: Bastille, 11ème
Address: 35 Rue De La Roquette
75011 Paris France
Phone: 01 49 29 00 50

#122
Nina Kendosa
Category: Women's Clothing, Accessories
Average Price: Modest
Area: 4ème, Île De La Cité/Île Saint Louis
Address: 43 Rue Saint-Louis-En-L'île
75004 Paris France
Phone: 01 43 26 59 86

#123
Shanghai Lafayette
Category: Women's Clothing
Average Price: Modest
Area: Chaussée d'Antin, 9ème
Address: 17 Route La Fayette
75009 Paris France
Phone: 01 42 80 29 48

#124
Noix De Coco
Category: Accessories,
Women's Clothing, Tea Rooms
Average Price: Exclusive
Area: Canal St Martin/Gare De l'Est, 10ème
Address: 59 Rue De Lancry
75010 Paris France
Phone: 01 42 40 10 33

#125
Intemporel
Category: Antiques, Home Decor
Average Price: Modest
Area: Beaubourg, 4ème
Address: 22 Rue St Martin
75004 Paris France
Phone: 01 42 72 55 41

#126
Pep's
Category: Arts & Crafts, Accessories
Average Price: Modest
Area: Arts & Métiers/Rambuteau, 3ème
Address: 223 Rue St Martin
75003 Paris France
Phone: 01 42 78 11 67

#127
Atelier Couronnes
Category: Shoe Stores, Accessories, Jewelry
Average Price: Modest
Area: République
Address: 6 Rue Du Château d'Eau
75010 Paris France
Phone: 01 40 37 03 54

#128
Louis Vuitton
Category: Leather Goods, Men's Clothing
Average Price: Exclusive
Area: Saint-Germain-Des-Prés, 6ème
Address: 170 Boulevard Saint-Germain
75006 Paris France
Phone: 01 45 49 62 32

#129
Fauré Le Page
Category: Accessories
Average Price: Exclusive
Area: Concorde/Madeleine
Address: 21 Rue Cambon
75001 Paris France
Phone: 01 49 27 99 36

#130
Oxyde
Category: Women's Clothing
Average Price: Expensive
Area: Beaubourg, Marais, 4ème
Address: 7 Rue Saint Merri
75004 Paris France
Phone: 01 42 77 34 54

#131
Delphine Pariente
Category: Women's Clothing,
Jewelry, Accessories
Average Price: Expensive
Area: Marais Nord, 3ème, Marais
Address: 101 Rue De Turenne
75004 Paris France
Phone: 01 42 78 18 87

#132
Room Service
Category: Women's Clothing
Average Price: Expensive
Area: Etienne Marcel/Montorgueil, 2ème
Address: 52 Rue Argout
75002 Paris France
Phone: 01 77 11 27 24

#133
Longchamp
Category: Leather Goods
Average Price: Expensive
Area: 6ème, Saint-Germain-Des-Prés
Address: 21 Rue Du Vieux Colombier
75006 Paris France
Phone: 01 42 22 74 75

#134
London Styl '
Category: Men's Clothing, Women's Clothing
Average Price: Expensive
Area: 15ème, Vaugirard/Grenelle
Address:
75 Boulevard Grenelle
75015 Paris France
Phone: 01 47 34 00 15

#135
Y'en A Que Pour Lui
Category: Gift Shops
Average Price: Inexpensive
Area: Montmartre, 18ème
Address: 5 Rue Lepic
75018 Paris France
Phone: 01 46 06 90 58

#136
Hermine De Pashmina
Category: Women's Clothing, Men's Clothing
Average Price: Modest
Area: Vaugirard/Grenelle, 15ème
Address: 154 Ave Emile Zola
75015 Paris France
Phone: 01 45 79 76 42

#137
Mango
Category: Women's Clothing
Average Price: Modest
Area: Châtelet/Les Halles, 4ème
Address: 82 Rue De Rivoli
75004 Paris France
Phone: 01 44 59 80 37

#138
El Indio Feliz
Category: Arts & Crafts, Accessories
Average Price: Modest
Area: Ledru-Rollin, 11ème
Address: 69 Rue Roquette
75011 Paris France
Phone: 01 43 72 52 88

#139
Miss Sugar Cane
Category: Jewelry, Used, Vintage &
Consignment, Accessories
Average Price: Expensive
Area: Batignolles, 17ème
Address: 43 Rue Des Dames
75017 Paris France
Phone: 09 66 94 15 97

#140
Monoprix
Category: Department Stores
Average Price: Modest
Area: Arts & Métiers/Rambuteau, 2ème
Address: 95 Bd Sébastopol
75002 Paris France
Phone: 01 42 33 36 15

#141
Celio
Category: Men's Clothing, Accessories
Average Price: Modest
Area: Châtelet/Les Halles, 1er
Address: 49 Rue De Rivoli
75001 Paris France
Phone: 01 40 28 44 82

#142
Extrovert
Category: Fashion
Average Price: Modest
Area: Saint-Michel/Odéon, 6ème
Address: 47 Rue St André Des Arts
75006 Paris France
Phone: 01 75 51 28 68

#143
Médecine Douce
Category: Accessories, Jewelry
Average Price: Expensive
Area: Canal St Martin/Gare De l'Est, 10ème
Address: 10 Rue Marseille
75010 Paris France
Phone: 01 48 03 57 28

#144
Somewhere
Category: Women's Clothing
Average Price: Modest
Area: 15ème, Vaugirard/Grenelle
Address: 93 Rue Commerce
75015 Paris France
Phone: 01 48 56 17 78

#145
The Kooples
Category: Men's Clothing, Women's Clothing
Average Price: Exclusive
Area: Marais, 4ème
Address: 31 Rue Rosiers
75004 Paris France
Phone: 01 42 78 75 38

#146
Défilé De Marques
Category: Used, Vintage & Consignment,
Leather Goods, Shoe Stores
Average Price: Modest
Area: Tour Eiffel/Champ De Mars, 7ème
Address: 171 Rue De Grenelle
75007 Paris France
Phone: 06 64 18 63 47

#147
Nikita
Category: Women's Clothing
Average Price: Modest
Area: Bastille, 11ème
Address: 7 Rue De La Roquette
75011 Paris France
Phone: 01 47 00 85 48

#148
Muji
Category: Home Decor, Furniture Stores,
Kitchen & Bath
Average Price: Modest
Area: Denfert-Rochereau, 14ème
Address: 32 Avenue Du Général Leclerc
75014 Paris France
Phone: 01 43 95 60 72

#149
L'Eclaireur
Category: Men's Clothing, Accessories,
Women's Clothing
Average Price: Expensive
Area: Bourse, 1er
Address: 10 Rue Hérold
75001 Paris France
Phone: 01 40 41 09 89

#150
Longchamp
Category: Accessories, Shoe Stores
Average Price: Exclusive
Area: Champs-Elysées, 8ème
Address: 77 Avenue Des Champs-Élysées
75008 Paris France
Phone: 01 53 76 27 76

#151
Tom Greyhound
Category: Women's Clothing, Men's Clothing
Average Price: Expensive
Area: Marais Nord, 3ème, Marais
Address: 19 Rue De Saintonge
75003 Paris France
Phone: 01 44 61 36 59

#152
Anne Et Marion
Category: Women's Clothing
Average Price: Modest
Area: Batignolles, 17ème
Address: 58 Rue Dames
75017 Paris France
Phone: 01 42 93 33 19

#153
Le Sourire Multicolore
Category: Home Decor, Accessories,
Women's Clothing
Average Price: Modest
Area: 9ème, Richelieu-Drouot
Address: 13 Rue De Maubeuge
75009 Paris France
Phone: 01 40 16 82 32

#154
La Fabrique De Gepetto
Category: Toy Stores, Gift Shops
Average Price: Modest
Area: 5ème, Port Royal/Gobelins
Address: 50 Rue Daubenton
75005 Paris France
Phone: 01 45 35 18 57

#155
Hema
Category: Department Stores
Average Price: Inexpensive
Area: Europe/Miromesnil, 8ème
Address: 1 Cour De Rome
75008 Paris France
Phone: 01 42 93 88 08

#156
Vintage 77
Category: Used, Vintage & Consignment
Average Price: Modest
Area: Belleville/Ménilmontant, 20ème
Address: 77 Rue Ménilmontant
75020 Paris France
Phone: 01 47 97 77 17

#157
Nin & Laur
Category: Shoe Stores, Women's Clothing
Average Price: Modest
Area: Ledru-Rollin, 11ème
Address: 59 Rue De La Roquette
75011 Paris France
Phone: 09 67 50 79 58

#158
Autour Du Monde
Category: Women's Clothing,
Men's Clothing, Shoe Stores
Average Price: Modest
Area: Marais, 3ème
Address: 12 Rue Des Francs Bourgeois
75003 Paris France
Phone: 01 42 77 16 18

#159
Christian Louboutin
Category: Shoe Stores
Average Price: Exclusive
Area: Palais Royal/Musée Du Louvre, 1er
Address: 19 Rue Jean-Jacques Rousseau
75001 Paris France
Phone: 01 44 82 03 88

#160
Pop Market
Category: Home Decor, Flowers & Gifts
Average Price: Modest
Area: Canal St Martin/Gare De l'Est, 10ème
Address: 50 Rue Bichat
75010 Paris France
Phone: 09 52 79 96 86

#161
Vanina Escoubet
Category: Women's Clothing, Accessories
Average Price: Expensive
Area: Pigalle, 9ème
Address: 1 Rue Henry Monnier
75009 Paris France
Phone: 01 42 74 31 42

#162
Promod
Category: Women's Clothing
Average Price: Modest
Area: Châtelet/Les Halles, 1er
Address: 110 Rue De Rivoli
75001 Paris France
Phone: 01 40 39 09 24

#163
K.B Stock
Category: Fashion, Outlet Stores
Average Price: Modest
Area: Auteuil, 16ème
Address: 2 Rue Duban
75016 Paris France
Phone: 01 45 24 68 01

#164
Dealer
Category: Used, Vintage & Consignment
Average Price: Modest
Area: Mairie Du 18e/Lamarck, 18ème
Address: 15 Rue Lapeyrere
75018 Paris France
Phone: 01 42 62 35 77

#165
Capsule Tokyo
Category: Accessories, Men's Clothing,
Women's Clothing
Average Price: Modest
Area: Ledru-Rollin, Bastille, 11ème
Address: 27 Rue Taillandiers
75011 Paris France
Phone: 09 62 61 64 29

#166
Les Nguyen
Category: Women's Clothing, Accessories
Average Price: Modest
Area: 4ème, Marais
Address: 12 Rue St Paul
75004 Paris France
Phone: 01 44 61 29 46

#167
Authentique Parenthèse
Category: Accessories, Home Decor
Average Price: Modest
Area: Belleville/Ménilmontant, 20ème
Address: 50 Rue De La Bidassoa
75020 PARIS 20 France
Phone: 01 72 60 91 88

#168
Mision Misericordia
Category: Men's Clothing, Women's Clothing
Average Price: Modest
Area: Bastille, 11ème
Address: 7-9 Rue De Charonne
75011 Paris France
Phone: 09 54 67 98 66

#169
Mansaya
Category: Women's Clothing, Accessories
Average Price: Modest
Area: Ledru-Rollin, 11ème
Address: 49 Rue Léon Frot
75011 Paris France
Phone: 01 71 26 71 73

#170
Monoprix
Category: Grocery
Average Price: Modest
Area: Montparnasse, 14ème
Address: 31 Rue Du Départ
75014 Paris France
Phone: 01 43 20 69 30

#171
Antoine Et Lili
Category: Women's Clothing
Average Price: Expensive
Area: Marais, Marais Nord, 4ème
Address: 51 Rue Des Francs Bourgeois
75004 Paris France
Phone: 01 42 72 26 60

#172
Monoprix
Category: Department Stores
Average Price: Modest
Area: Saint-Germain-Des-Prés, 6ème
Address: 52 Rue De Rennes
75006 Paris France
Phone: 01 45 48 18 08

#173
Monoprix
Category: Department Stores
Average Price: Modest
Area: Musée d'Orsay, 7ème
Address: 35 Rue Du Bac
75007 Paris France
Phone: 01 42 86 44 30

#174
& Other Stories
Category: Fashion
Average Price: Modest
Area: Concorde/Madeleine, 8ème
Address: 277 Rue Saint-Honoré
75008 Paris France
Phone: 01 53 32 85 05

#175
Mamie
Category: Used, Vintage &
Consignment, Thrift Stores
Average Price: Modest
Area: 9ème
Address: 73 Rue De Rochechouart
75009 Paris France
Phone: 01 42 82 09 98

#176
Kitsuné
Category: Coffee & Tea, Fashion
Average Price: Expensive
Area: Pigalle, 9ème
Address: 68 Rue Condorcet
75009 Paris France
Phone: 01 45 26 11 64

#177
Le Marché Franprix
Category: Department Stores
Average Price: Modest
Area: 15ème
Address: 405 Rue Vaugirard
75015 Paris France
Phone: 01 48 28 57 83

#178
Forever 21
Category: Women's Clothing, Men's Clothing
Average Price: Inexpensive
Area: Châtelet/Les Halles, 1er
Address: Forum Des Halles
75001 Paris France
Phone: 01 42 21 32 40

#179
Zara
Category: Men's Clothing, Women's Clothing
Average Price: Modest
Area: 8ème, Avenue Montaigne
Address: 44 Avenue Des Champs Elysées
75008 Paris France
Phone: 01 45 61 52 80

#180
Notify
Category: Men's Clothing, Women's Clothing
Average Price: Modest
Area: Place Vendôme
Address: 1-3 Rue Saint-Hyacinthe
75002 Paris France
Phone: 01 44 50 05 00

#181
Ultrason
Category: Shoe Stores, Men's Clothing
Average Price: Modest
Area: Châtelet/Les Halles, 1er
Address: 51 Rue Saint-Denis
75001 Paris France
Phone: 01 45 08 18 46

#182
Noblase
Category: Used, Vintage & Consignment
Average Price: Inexpensive
Area: Pigalle, 9ème
Address: 18 Rue Pierre Fontaine
75009 Paris France
Phone: 01 44 63 43 52

#183
La Halle Au Vêtement
Category: Women's Clothing,
Department Stores
Average Price: Modest
Area: La Villette, 19ème
Address: 26 Avenue De Flandre
75019 Paris France
Phone: 01 53 35 04 25

#184
Biba Boutique
Category: Fashion
Average Price: Expensive
Area: 6ème, Saint-Germain-Des-Prés, 7ème
Address: 18 Rue Sèvres
75007 Paris France
Phone: 01 42 22 10 14

#185
Bridget
Category: Women's Clothing
Average Price: Expensive
Area: 9ème, Pigalle
Address: 17 Rue Martyrs
75009 Paris France
Phone: 01 48 78 33 94

#186
Monoprix
Category: Department Stores
Average Price: Modest
Area: Strasbourg-St Denis/Bonne
Nouvelle, 10ème
Address: 91 Rue Fbg St Denis
75010 Paris France
Phone: 01 53 34 60 07

#187
Monoprix
Category: Department Stores
Average Price: Modest
Area: Palais Royal/Musée Du Louvre, 1er
Address: 23 Avenue De l'Opéra
75001 Paris France
Phone: 01 42 61 78 08

#188
La Salle Des Ventes Du Particulier
Category: Used, Vintage & Consignment
Average Price: Expensive
Area: La Villette, 19ème
Address: 63 Quai De Seine
75019 Paris France
Phone: 01 40 35 40 29

#189
Saga Des Marques
Category: Women's Clothing, Men's Clothing
Average Price: Inexpensive
Area: 14ème, Denfert-Rochereau
Address: 41 Avenue Du Général Leclerc
75014 Paris France
Phone: 01 40 17 06 84

#190
Libellune
Category: Arts & Crafts, Jewelry, Accessories
Average Price: Modest
Area: Batignolles, 17ème
Address: 80 Rue Legendre
75017 Paris France
Phone: 01 53 11 13 05

#191
Faguo
Category: Shoe Stores, Men's Clothing,
Women's Clothing
Average Price: Modest
Area: Marais, 3ème, Marais Nord
Address: 81 Rue Vieille Du Temple
75003 Paris France
Phone: 01 42 71 10 42

#192
Mini Nippes
Category: Used, Vintage & Consignment
Average Price: Modest
Area: Strasbourg-St Denis
Address: 4 Rue La Tour D'auvergne
75009 Paris France
Phone: 01 48 78 26 94

#193
Next Stop
Category: Men's Clothing
Average Price: Modest
Area: Saint-Michel/Odéon
Address: 58 Rue St André Des Arts
75006 Paris France
Phone: 01 56 24 43 21

#194
Promod
Category: Fashion
Average Price: Modest
Area: Malesherbes/Villiers, 17ème
Address: 29 Rue De Levis
75017 Paris France
Phone: 01 44 40 25 11

#195
AB33
Category: Women's Clothing, Accessories
Average Price: Modest
Area: Marais Nord, 3ème, Marais
Address: 33 Rue Charlot
75003 Paris France
Phone: 01 42 71 02 82

#196
Pépites
Category: Fashion
Average Price: Modest
Area: 3ème, Marais Nord, Arts &
Métiers/Rambuteau, Marais
Address: 327 Rue St Martin
75003 Paris France
Phone: 01 48 87 65 60

#197
Les Sabots De Marie
Category: Shoe Stores, Accessories
Average Price: Modest
Area: Ledru-Rollin, 11ème
Address: 25 Rue Faidherbe
75011 Paris France
Phone: 01 43 67 06 60

#198
Roxan
Category: Women's Clothing
Average Price: Modest
Area: Montmartre, 18ème
Address: 25 Rue Lepic
75018 Paris France
Phone: 01 42 52 47 70

#199
Obliq
Category: Fashion
Average Price: Modest
Area: Arts & Métiers/Rambuteau, 3ème
Address: 157 Rue St Martin
75003 Paris France
Phone: 01 44 54 97 10

#200
Montaigne Market
Category: Men's Clothing, Women's Clothing
Average Price: Exclusive
Area: Avenue Montaigne
Address: 57 Ave Montaigne
75008 Paris France
Phone: 01 42 56 58 58

#201
Ambrym
Category: Women's Clothing,
Accessories
Average Price: Modest
Area: Canal St Martin/Gare De l'Est, 10ème
Address: 22-24 Rue Des Vinaigriers
75010 Paris France
Phone: 01 42 05 35 38

#202
Lei
Category: Women's Clothing
Average Price: Modest
Area: Palais Royal/Musée Du Louvre, 2ème
Address: 36 Rue Des Petits
Champs 75002 Paris France
Phone: 01 42 61 12 40

#203
Anne Willi
Category: Women's Clothing
Average Price: Expensive
Area: Ledru-Rollin, 11ème
Address: 13 Rue Keller
75011 Paris France
Phone: 01 48 06 74 06

#204
Valentine Gauthier
Category: Women's Clothing
Average Price: Expensive
Area: Marais Nord, 3ème
Address: 58 Rue Charlot
75003 Paris France
Phone: 01 48 87 68 40

#205
**Maison Martin
Margiela - Boutique Femme**
Category: Women's Clothing
Average Price: Exclusive
Area: Palais Royal/Musée Du Louvre, 1er
Address: 25 Bis Rue De Montpensier
75001 Paris France
Phone: 01 40 15 07 55

#206
Gant Rugger
Category: Women's Clothing,
Men's Clothing, Children's Clothing
Average Price: Modest
Area: Marais Nord, 3ème, Marais
Address: 116 Rue Vieille Du Temple
75003 Paris France
Phone: 01 42 74 80 02

#207
Kurochiku
Category: Arts & Crafts, Accessories, Jewelry
Average Price: Modest
Area: 4ème, Marais
Address: 50 Rue De l'Hotel De Ville
75004 Paris France
Phone: 01 42 77 44 80

#208
Gucci
Category: Shoe Stores, Accessories
Average Price: Exclusive
Area: Concorde/Madeleine, 8ème
Address: 2 Rue Du Faubourg St Honoré
75008 Paris France
Phone: 01 44 94 14 70

#209
La Fée Maraboutée
Category: Women's Clothing
Average Price: Expensive
Area: Bastille, 11ème
Address: 5 Rue Charonne
75011 Paris France
Phone: 01 48 05 97 89

#210
Kitsuné
Category: Books, Mags, Music & Video,
Men's Clothing, Women's Clothing
Average Price: Expensive
Area: Palais Royal/Musée Du Louvre, 1er
Address: 52 Rue De Richelieu
75001 Paris France
Phone: 01 42 60 34 28

#211
Tati
Category: Women's Clothing,
Men's Clothing, Discount Store
Average Price: Inexpensive
Area: Barbès/Goutte d'Or, 18ème
Address: 4 Bd Rochechouart
75018 Paris France
Phone: 01 55 29 50 00

#212
La Petite Boutique De Mode
Category: Women's Clothing
Average Price: Modest
Area: Oberkampf/Parmentier, 11ème
Address: 41 Avenue De La République
75011 Paris France
Phone: 01 48 05 27 26

#213
Kesslord
Category: Leather Goods,
Shoe Stores, Accessories
Average Price: Modest
Area: Arts & Métiers/Rambuteau, 3ème
Address: 65 Rue Beaubourg
75003 Paris France
Phone: 01 42 72 86 80

#214
Diwali
Category: Accessories
Average Price: Modest
Area: Montmartre, 18ème
Address: 5 Rue Norvins
75018 Paris France
Phone: 01 42 54 16 35

#215
La Petite Mendigote
Category: Accessories, Shoe Stores
Average Price: Modest
Area: Saint-Germain-Des-Prés, 6ème
Address: 23 Rue Dragon
75006 Paris France
Phone: 01 42 84 20 07

#216
Frenchtrotters
Category: Men's Clothing
Average Price: Expensive
Area: Ledru-Rollin, 11ème
Address: 30 Rue Charonne
75011 Paris France
Phone: 01 43 55 87 17

#217
Valentino
Category: Accessories, Women's Clothing
Average Price: Exclusive
Area: Concorde/Madeleine, 8ème
Address: 27 Rue Du Faubourg Saint-Honoré
75008 Paris France
Phone: 01 42 66 95 94

#218
Repetto
Category: Women's Clothing, Sports Wear
Average Price: Expensive
Area: Opéra, Place Vendôme, 2ème
Address: 22 Rue Paix
75002 Paris France
Phone: 01 44 71 83 12

#219
Moncler
Category: Women's Clothing, Men's Clothing
Average Price: Exclusive
Area: Concorde/Madeleine, 8ème
Address: 5 Rue Du Faubourg
Saint Honoré 75008 Paris France
Phone: 01 53 05 92 15

#220
Minute Papillon
Category: Accessories, Gift Shops
Average Price: Modest
Area: Vaugirard/Grenelle, 15ème
Address: 34 Rue Lecourbe
75015 Paris France
Phone: 01 45 66 79 45

#221
June & Jim
Category: Women's Clothing, Accessories
Average Price: Modest
Area: 9ème
Address: 69 Rue De Rochechouart
75009 Paris France
Phone: 01 40 23 08 05

#222
Forever 21
Category: Women's Clothing,
Accessories, Men's Clothing
Average Price: Modest
Area: Châtelet/Les Halles, 1er
Address: 144 Rue De Rivoli
75001 Paris France
Phone: 01 40 26 78 81

#223
Poodle
Category: Thrift Stores
Average Price: Inexpensive
Area: Bercy, 12ème
Address: 16 Rue Crozatier
75012 Paris France
Phone: 01 43 41 23 25

#224
Shanghai Tang
Category: Women's Clothing, Men's Clothing
Average Price: Expensive
Area: 6ème, Saint-Germain-Des-Prés
Address: 76 Rue Bonaparte
75006 Paris France
Phone: 01 40 51 95 16

#225
Suite 114
Category: Accessories, Women's Clothing
Average Price: Expensive
Area: Musée d'Orsay, 7ème
Address: 114 Rue Bac
75007 Paris France
Phone: 01 42 84 07 56

#226
Tiennette La Belette
Category: Fashion, Discount Store
Average Price: Modest
Area: Père Lachaise, 20ème
Address: 49 Rue Bagnolet
75020 Paris France
Phone: 01 44 64 77 67

#227
Chaussures Tavernier
Category: Shoe Stores
Average Price: Modest
Area: 5ème, Sorbonne/Panthéon
Address: 99 Rue Mouffetard
75005 Paris France
Phone: 01 45 35 17 71

#228
Zara
Category: Men's Clothing, Women's Clothing,
Children's Clothing
Average Price: Modest
Area: Denfert-Rochereau, 14ème
Address: 14 Avenue Du Général Leclerc
75014 Paris France
Phone: 01 40 64 00 13

#229
Devred
Category: Fashion
Average Price: Modest
Area: Grands Boulevards/Sentier, 2ème
Address: 14-16 Bd Poissonnières
75009 Paris France
Phone: 01 42 46 73 16

#230
La Clarière
Category: Home Decor, Fabric Stores, Linens
Average Price: Inexpensive
Area: Butte Aux Cailles
Address: 8 Rue De L'Espérance
75013 Paris France
Phone: 01 82 09 44 79

#231
L'auto École
Category: Jewelry, Accessories
Average Price: Expensive
Area: Oberkampf/Parmentier, 11ème
Address: 101 Rue Oberkampf
75011 Paris France
Phone: 01 43 55 31 94

#232
Nitya
Category: Women's Clothing
Average Price: Modest
Area: Saint-Germain-Des-Prés, 6ème
Address: 40 Rue Bonaparte
75006 Paris France
Phone: 01 42 61 96 30

#233
Chez Chiffons Vintage
Category: Used, Vintage & Consignment
Average Price: Modest
Area: Canal St Martin/Gare De l'Est, 10ème
Address: 47 Rue De Lancry
75010 Paris France
Phone: 06 20 73 30 23

#234
Bock De Boheme
Category: Fashion
Average Price: Inexpensive
Area: Montparnasse, 14ème
Address: 104 Rue Du Chateau
75014 Paris France
Phone: 01 43 22 62 96

#235
Folies A Faire
Category: Department Stores
Average Price: Modest
Area: 17ème
Address: 34 Rue Jouffroy d'Abbans
75017 Paris France
Phone: 01 46 22 28 86

#236
Pigalle
Category: Fashion
Average Price: Expensive
Area: Pigalle, 9ème
Address: 7 Rue Henry Monnier
75009 Paris France
Phone: 01 48 78 59 74

#237
Lanvin
Category: Women's Clothing
Average Price: Exclusive
Area: Concorde/Madeleine, 8ème
Address: 22 Rue Du Faubourg St Honore
75008 Paris France
Phone: 01 44 71 33 33

#238
Nafnaf
Category: Women's Clothing
Average Price: Modest
Area: Champs-Elysées, 8ème
Address: 62-68 Ave Des Champs
Élysées 75008 Paris France
Phone: 01 45 62 03 08

#239
Céline
Category: Fashion
Average Price: Exclusive
Area: Avenue Montaigne
Address: 36 Avenue Montaigne
75008 Paris France
Phone: 01 56 89 07 92

#240
Come Back
Category: Vintage & Consignment
Average Price: Modest
Area: Père Lachaise, 20ème
Address: 51 Rue Des Orteaux
75020 Paris France
Phone: 06 85 07 46 96

#241
Kate Mack
Category: Women's Clothing
Average Price: Modest
Area: 11ème
Address: 15 Rue Oberkampf
75011 Paris France
Phone: 01 48 07 08 41

#242
Monoprix
Category: Grocery, Fashion, Perfume
Average Price: Modest
Area: Buttes Chaumont, 19ème
Address: 7 Et 16 Avenue Secretan
75019 Paris France
Phone: 01 42 38 27 50

#243
Crimson
Category: Fashion
Average Price: Modest
Area: Champs-Elysées, 8ème
Address: 8 Rue Marbeuf
75008 Paris France
Phone: 01 47 20 44 24

#244
Long Time
Category: Fashion
Average Price: Modest
Area: 14ème
Address: 107 Avenue Gén Leclerc
75014 Paris France
Phone: 01 45 41 72 83

#245
Elégance
Category: Fashion
Average Price: Modest
Area: Guy Moquet/Saint Ouen, 17ème
Address: 77 Avenue De Clichy
75017 Paris France
Phone: 01 42 26 73 15

#246
Monoprix
Category: Department Stores
Average Price: Modest
Area: Saint-Lazare/Grands Magasins, 9ème
Address: 47 Rue De Caumartin
75009 Paris France
Phone: 01 44 53 79 79

#247
BHV
Category: Shopping Centers
Average Price: Expensive
Area: Beaubourg, Marais, 4ème
Address: 42 Rue De La Verrerie
75004 Paris France
Phone: 09 77 40 14 00

#248
Comptoir Des Cotonniers
Category: Women's Clothing
Average Price: Expensive
Area: 7ème, Tour Eiffel/Champ De Mars
Address: 78 Rue St Dominique
75007 Paris France
Phone: 01 47 53 06 38

#249
Christian Louboutin
Category: Shoe Stores
Average Price: Expensive
Area: Saint-Germain-Des-Prés, 7ème
Address: 38/40 Rue De Grenelle
75007 Paris France
Phone: 01 42 22 33 07

#250
Gabrielle Geppert
Category: Women's Clothing, Leather Goods,
Used, Vintage & Consignment
Average Price: Exclusive
Area: Palais Royal/Musée Du Louvre, 1er
Address: 31 & 34 Galerie Montpensier
75001 Paris France
Phone: 01 42 61 53 52

#251
Dussica
Category: Fashion
Average Price: Modest
Area: Montmartre, 18ème
Address: 11 Rue La Vieuville
75018 Paris France
Phone: 01 42 23 78 22

#252
Manoush
Category: Women's Clothing, Accessories
Average Price: Expensive
Area: Saint-Germain-Des-Prés, 6ème
Address: 52 Rue Du Four
75006 Paris France
Phone: 01 42 22 78 45

#253
Agnès B. Femme
Category: Women's Clothing
Average Price: Modest
Area: 6ème, Saint-Germain-Des-Prés
Address: 6 Rue Du Vieux Colombier
75006 Paris France
Phone: 01 44 39 02 60

#254
Sensitive Et Fils
Category: Home Decor, Women's
Clothing, Furniture Stores
Average Price: Expensive
Area: Ledru-Rollin, 11ème
Address: 31 Rue Faidherbe
75011 Paris France
Phone: 01 43 72 33 96

#255
Les Tambours De Bronze
Category: Accessories, Home Decor
Average Price: Modest
Area: Jardin Des Plantes/Austerlitz, 5ème
Address: 25 Rue Geoffroy Saint Hilaire
75005 Paris France
Phone: 01 55 43 85 69

#256
Les Halles De L'Asie
Category: Department Stores
Average Price: Inexpensive
Area: Colonel Fabien/Goncourt, 19ème
Address: 19 Rue Belleville
75019 Paris France
Phone: 01 42 38 18 98

#257
Patricia Louisor
Category: Fashion
Average Price: Modest
Area: Montmartre, Pigalle, 18ème
Address: 16 Rue Houdon
75018 Paris France
Phone: 01 42 62 10 42

#258
French Californians
Category: Fashion
Average Price: Expensive
Area: Etienne Marcel/Montorgueil, 2ème
Address: 19 Rue Tiquetonne
75002 Paris France
Phone: 01 42 33 02 49

#259
Bee'Shoes
Category: Shoe Stores
Average Price: Modest
Area: Strasbourg-St Denis
Address: 127 Rue La Fayette
75010 Paris France
Phone: 01 42 81 50 58

#260
Miss Coquines Paris
Category: Accessories
Average Price: Inexpensive
Area: Châtelet/Les Halles, 1er
Address: 78 Rue St Denis
75001 Paris France
Phone: 01 44 88 99 75

#261
Blue Lemon
Category: Accessories
Average Price: Modest
Area: Saint-Germain-Des-Prés
Address: 65 Rue Saint-André Des Arts
75006 Paris France
Phone: 01 46 33 17 51

#262
Kenzo
Category: Department Stores
Average Price: Expensive
Area: Concorde/Madeleine, 8ème
Address: 10 Place Madeleine
75008 Paris France
Phone: 01 42 61 04 14

#263
La Clef Des Marques
Category: Men's Clothing,
Women's Clothing
Average Price: Inexpensive
Area: Montparnasse, 6ème
Address: 124-126 Boulevard Raspail
75006 Paris France
Phone: 01 45 49 31 00

#264
Idécostore
Category: Jewelry, Accessories, Home Decor
Average Price: Modest
Area: Belleville/Ménilmontant, 19ème
Address: 103 Rue De Belleville
75020 Paris France
Phone: 01 42 06 35 30

#265
Fragonard
Category: Gift Shops, Perfume
Average Price: Modest
Area: Marais, Marais Nord, 4ème
Address: 51 Rue Francs Bourgeois
75004 Paris France
Phone: 01 44 78 01 32

#266
Bella Chic
Category: Women's Clothing
Average Price: Modest
Area: Colonel Fabien/Goncourt, 19ème
Address: 45 Rue Belleville
75019 Paris France
Phone: 01 42 02 95 14

#267
Urban Outfitters
Category: Men's Clothing,
Women's Clothing, Home Decor
Average Price: Expensive
Area: 9ème
Address: 40 Bd Haussmann
75009 Paris France
Phone: 01 42 82 34 56

#268
Noche De Abril
Category: Women's Clothing, Jewelry
Average Price: Modest
Area: Place De Clichy, Batignolles, 17ème
Address: 26 Rue Des Dames
75017 Paris France
Phone: 01 43 87 49 97

#269
Publicis Drugstore
Category: Shopping Centers
Average Price: Expensive
Area: Champs-Elysées, 8ème
Address: 133 Avenue Des Champs-Elysées
75008 Paris France
Phone: 01 44 43 79 00

#270
Bimba & Lola
Category: Shoe Stores,
Women's Clothing, Accessories
Average Price: Modest
Area: Marais, 4ème
Address: 17 Rue Pavée
75004 Paris France
Phone: 01 42 74 65 41

#271
Les Expressives
Category: Jewelry, Leather
Goods, Accessories
Average Price: Modest
Area: Beaubourg, 3ème
Address: 19 Passage Molière
75003 Paris France
Phone: 09 80 93 49 95

#272
Vanessa Bruno
Category: Women's Clothing
Average Price: Modest
Area: Saint-Germain-Des-Prés, 6ème
Address: 25 Rue St Sulpice
75006 Paris France
Phone: 01 43 54 41 04

#273
Anis
Category: Women's Clothing
Average Price: Inexpensive
Area: Victor Hugo, 16ème
Address: 149 Rue Pompe
75016 Paris France
Phone: 01 47 04 99 57

#274
Toumain
Category: Jewelry
Average Price: Inexpensive
Area: Canal St Martin/Gare De l'Est, 10ème
Address: 56 Rue Lancry
75010 Paris France
Phone: 01 42 03 63 22

#275
Showroom 23
Category: Jewelry, Women's Clothing
Average Price: Modest
Area: Ledru-Rollin, 11ème
Address: 23 Rue Faidherbe
75011 Paris France
Phone: 01 43 56 82 20

#276
Bijoux Cocktails
Category: Jewelry, Accessories,
Jewelry Repair
Average Price: Modest
Area: Saint-Michel/Odéon, 6ème
Address: 13 Rue Racine
75006 Paris France
Phone: 01 43 26 34 03

#277
Stock Cop.Copine
Category: Women's Clothing
Average Price: Modest
Area: Ledru-Rollin, 11ème
Address: 99 Rue Charonne
75011 Paris France
Phone: 01 43 70 26 33

#278
Leon & Harper
Category: Women's Clothing
Average Price: Exclusive
Area: Marais Nord, Marais, 3ème
Address: 95 Bd Beaumarchais
75003 Paris France
Phone: 01 42 71 25 01

#279
Boutique Onze
Category: Women's Clothing,
Accessories, Shoe Stores
Average Price: Modest
Area: 11ème
Address: 11 Rue Oberkampf
75011 Paris France
Phone: 01 43 55 32 11

#280
Jyvé Stock
Category: Men's Clothing, Women's Clothing
Average Price: Modest
Area: 12ème, Bercy
Address: 35 Bd De Reuilly
75012 Paris France
Phone: 01 46 28 23 53

#281
Fragonard
Category: Gift Shops, Perfume
Average Price: Modest
Area: Saint-Germain-Des-Prés, 7ème
Address: 196 Boulevard Saint-Germain
75006 Paris France
Phone: 01 42 84 12 12

#282
Eleven Paris
Category: Men's Clothing, Women's Clothing
Average Price: Modest
Area: Etienne Marcel/Montorgueil, 2ème
Address: 32 Rue Etienne Marcel
75002 Paris France
Phone: 01 42 33 30 64

#283
L'Habibliotheque
Category: Accessories, Women's Clothing
Average Price: Modest
Area: Marais Nord, 3ème
Address: 61 Rue De Saintonge
75003 Paris France
Phone: 09 81 43 43 43

#284
Les Trois Quartiers
Category: Shopping Centers,
Department Stores
Average Price: Modest
Area: Concorde/Madeleine, 9ème
Address: 23 Boulevard De La Madeleine
75009 Paris France
Phone: 01 42 97 80 12

#285
Loft, Design By
Category: Fashion
Average Price: Modest
Area: Marais, 4ème
Address: 12 Rue De Sévigné
75004 Paris France
Phone: 01 48 87 13 17

#286
L'Embellie
Category: Used, Vintage & Consignment
Average Price: Modest
Area: Tour Eiffel/Champ De Mars, 7ème
Address: 45 Avenue La Bourdonnais
75007 Paris France
Phone: 01 47 05 70 63

#287
Cé Pour Vous
Category: Jewelry, Accessories
Average Price: Modest
Area: Montparnasse, 14ème
Address: 81 Rue Daguerre
75014 Paris France
Phone: 09 80 49 42 11

#288
Les Billes De La Gamine
Category: Used, Vintage & Consignment
Average Price: Expensive
Area: Montmartre, Pigalle, 18ème
Address: 60 Rue d'Orsel
75018 Paris France
Phone: 01 77 11 14 13

#289
Bershka
Category: Women's Clothing, Men's Clothing
Average Price: Inexpensive
Area: Châtelet/Les Halles, 1er
Address: 101 Porte Berger
75001 Paris France
Phone: 01 40 28 10 22

#290
Chaussures André
Category: Shoe Stores, Accessories
Average Price: Expensive
Area: Châtelet/Les Halles, 1er
Address: 106 Rue Rivoli
75001 Paris France
Phone: 01 53 40 96 84

#291
Anne Maissoneuve
Category: Accessories, Screen
Printing/T-Shirt Printing
Average Price: Modest
Area: 6ème, Montparnasse
Address: 112 Boulevard Raspail
75006 Paris France
Phone: 01 42 22 42 70

#292
Chic Et Mignonne
Category: Bridal, Women's
Clothing, Accessories
Average Price: Inexpensive
Area: Grands Boulevards/Sentier, 2ème
Address: 123 Rue d'Aboukir
75002 Paris France
Phone: 01 42 33 08 73

#293
Altermundi
Category: Fashion, Home Decor
Average Price: Modest
Area: Mairie Du 18e/Lamarck, 18ème
Address: 135 Rue Ordener
75018 Paris France
Phone: 01 42 51 43 17

#294
The French Factory
Category: Accessories
Average Price: Modest
Area: La Villette, 19ème
Address: 131 Avenue De Flandre
75019 Paris France
Phone: 01 46 07 20 61

#295
Lilith
Category: Women's Clothing
Average Price: Expensive
Area: 6ème, Saint-Germain-Des-Prés
Address: 12 Rue Cherche Midi
75006 Paris France
Phone: 01 42 84 05 88

#296
Velvetine
Category: Leather Goods,
Jewelry, Women's Clothing
Average Price: Expensive
Area: Nation/Vincennes, 12ème
Address: 18 Rue Claude Tillier
75012 Paris France
Phone: 06 60 87 50 57

#297
Soleil d'Asie
Category: Jewelry, Women's Clothing
Average Price: Modest
Area: Place d'Italie, 13ème
Address: 130 Rue Tolbiac
75013 Paris France
Phone: 01 45 86 09 82

#298
Côte À Côte
Category: Women's Clothing
Average Price: Modest
Area: Champs-Elysées, 17ème
Address: 25 Ave De Wagram
75017 Paris France
Phone: 01 43 80 39 39

#299
Gelati, Lemoine Guylaine
Category: Shoe Stores
Average Price: Expensive
Area: Marais, 3ème, Marais Nord
Address: 75 Rue Vieille Du Temple
75003 Paris France
Phone: 01 42 71 37 75

#300
Robin Des Jeux
Category: Toy Stores
Average Price: Modest
Area: Nation/Vincennes
Address: 37 Bd De Charonne
75011 Paris France
Phone: 07 82 54 28 33

#301
Africouleur
Category: Men's Clothing, Women's Clothing
Average Price: Modest
Area: Oberkampf/Parmentier, 11ème
Address: 108 Rue St Maur
75011 Paris France
Phone: 01 56 98 15 36

#302
Terry Lane
Category: Women's Clothing
Average Price: Modest
Area: Grands Boulevards/Sentier, Etienne Marcel/Montorgueil, 2ème
Address: 40 Rue Des Petits Carreaux
75002 Paris France
Phone: 09 54 09 93 12

#303
Croix Rouge Française Comité 10
Category: Women's Clothing, Bookstores
Average Price: Inexpensive
Area: République, Canal St Martin
Address: 40 Rue Albert Thomas
75010 Paris France
Phone: 01 42 06 79 05

#304
Limi Feu
Category: Women's Clothing
Average Price: Modest
Area: Etienne Marcel/Montorgueil, 1er
Address: 25 Rue Du Louvre
75001 Paris France
Phone: 01 45 08 82 45

#305
Petites Chéries
Category: Women's Clothing, Accessories
Average Price: Modest
Area: Pigalle, 9ème
Address: 17 Rue Henry Monnier
75009 Paris France
Phone: 01 45 26 09 03

#306
L'Appartement
Category: Accessories, Home Decor
Average Price: Modest
Area: 1er, Palais Royal/Musée Du Louvre
Address: 99 Rue De Rivoli
75001 Paris France
Phone: 01 40 20 07 84

#307
Markowski Chausseur
Category: Shoe Stores
Average Price: Modest
Area: Strasbourg-St Denis
Address: 46 Rue De Paradis
75010 Paris France
Phone: 01 48 00 83 07

#308
Zazoubara
Category: Home Decor, Children's Clothing
Average Price: Modest
Area: 20ème
Address: 13 Av Du Père Lachaise
75020 Paris France
Phone: 01 46 36 08 20

#309
Monoprix
Category: Bakeries, Fashion
Average Price: Expensive
Area: Saint-Germain-Des-Prés, 6ème
Address: 10 Rue Bernard Palissy
75006 Paris France
Phone: 01 45 44 34 95

#310
Nilaï
Category: Accessories, Jewelry
Average Price: Modest
Area: Marais, 4ème
Address: 2 Rue Des Rosiers
75004 Paris France
Phone: 01 84 16 17 58

#311
Le 66
Category: Women's Clothing, Men's Clothing, Concept Shops
Average Price: Expensive
Area: 8ème, Avenue Montaigne
Address: 66 Avenue Des Champs-Elysées
75008 Paris France
Phone: 01 53 53 33 80

#312
Exclusif
Category: Shoe Stores, Accessories
Average Price: Modest
Area: Auteuil, 16ème
Address: 33 Rue Auteuil
75016 Paris France
Phone: 01 45 24 01 10

#313
Carrefour Market
Category: Department Stores
Average Price: Modest
Area: Butte Aux Cailles, Place d'Italie, 13ème
Address: 174 Rue De Tolbiac
75013 Paris France
Phone: 01 53 62 80 30

#314
COS
Category: Women's Clothing, Men's Clothing
Average Price: Expensive
Area: Etienne Marcel/Montorgueil, 2ème
Address: 68 Rue Montmartre
75002 Paris France
Phone: 01 55 80 52 00

#315
Act'2
Category: Men's Clothing
Average Price: Modest
Area: Montmartre, Pigalle, 18ème
Address: 2 Rue Des Trois Frères
75018 Paris France
Phone: 01 42 54 01 56

#316
Le Repère
Category: Women's Clothing,
Tea Rooms, Breakfast & Brunch
Average Price: Modest
Area: Canal St Martin/Gare De l'Est, 10ème
Address: 29 Rue Beaurepaire
75010 Paris France
Phone: 01 42 01 41 20

#317
La Cour
Category: Women's Clothing
Average Price: Modest
Area: Etienne Marcel/Montorgueil, 2ème
Address: 60 Rue Tiquetonne
75002 Paris France
Phone: 01 40 39 00 07

#318
Made By Moi
Category: Accessories,
Women's Clothing, Jewelry
Average Price: Expensive
Area: Oberkampf/Parmentier, 11ème
Address: 86 Rue Oberkampf
75011 Paris France
Phone: 01 58 30 95 78

#319
Tienda Esquipulas
Category: Arts & Crafts
Average Price: Inexpensive
Area: Montmartre, Pigalle, 18ème
Address: 20 Rue Houdon
75018 Paris France
Phone: 09 63 62 11 91

#320
Marie Mercié
Category: Arts & Crafts, Accessories
Average Price: Exclusive
Area: Saint-Germain-Des-Prés, 6ème
Address: 23 Rue St Sulpice
75006 Paris France
Phone: 01 43 26 45 83

#321
Mango
Category: Women's Clothing, Men's Clothing
Average Price: Modest
Area: Saint-Lazare/Grands Magasins, 9ème
Address: 54 Bd Haussmann
75009 Paris France
Phone: 01 44 53 73 30

#322
L'Eventail
Category: Used, Vintage &
Consignment, Antiques
Average Price: Modest
Area: Trocadéro/Iéna, 16ème
Address: 65 Bis Rue Lauriston
75116 Paris France
Phone: 01 47 04 58 68

#323
Sessùn
Category: Women's Clothing,
Accessories, Home Decor
Average Price: Expensive
Area: Ledru-Rollin, 11ème
Address: 34 Rue De Charonne
75011 Paris France
Phone: 01 48 06 55 66

#324
Guerrisol
Category: Used, Vintage & Consignment
Average Price: Inexpensive
Area: Ledru-Rollin, 12ème
Address: 45 Boulevard De La Chapelle
75018 Paris France
Phone: 01 49 95 93 86

#325
Lulu Berlu
Category: Toy Stores, Antiques
Average Price: Exclusive
Area: Oberkampf/Parmentier, 11ème
Address: 2 Rue Grand-Prieuré
75011 Paris France
Phone: 01 43 55 12 52

#326
Objet Céleste
Category: Jewelry, Accessories
Average Price: Modest
Area: Colonel Fabien/Goncourt, 10ème
Address: 25 Rue Bichat
75010 Paris France
Phone: 01 72 60 80 79

#327
Bonton
Category: Children's Clothing,
Toy Stores
Average Price: Expensive
Area: Marais Nord, 3ème, Marais
Address: 5 Bd Des Filles Du Calvaire
75003 Paris France
Phone: 01 42 72 34 69

#328
Kulte
Category: Men's Clothing,
Women's Clothing
Average Price: Modest
Area: Ledru-Rollin, 11ème
Address: 35 Rue De Charonne
75011 Paris France
Phone: 01 48 05 68 35

#329
Ba & Sh
Category: Women's Clothing
Average Price: Modest
Area: Marais, 4ème
Address: 22 Rue Des Francs Bourgeois
75003 Paris France
Phone: 01 42 78 55 10

#330
By Mutation
Category: Fashion
Average Price: Modest
Area: Belleville/Ménilmontant, 20ème
Address: 30 Rue Etienne Dolet
75020 Paris France
Phone: 01 43 49 23 52

#331
H&M
Category: Women's Clothing, Men's Clothing
Average Price: Inexpensive
Area: Saint-Lazare/Grands Magasins, 9ème
Address: 96 Rue De Provence
75009 Paris France
Phone: 01 53 32 85 00

#332
Camille & R
Category: Jewelry, Leather Goods,
Accessories
Average Price: Modest
Area: Malesherbes/Villiers, 17ème
Address: 81 Rue De Lévis
75017 Paris France
Phone: 01 47 63 12 46

#333
Burberry
Category: Women's Clothing,
Men's Clothing, Accessories
Average Price: Modest
Area: Concorde/Madeleine, 8ème
Address: 8 Boulevard Malesherbes
75008 Paris France
Phone: 01 47 07 77 77

#334
Nike Running
Category: Shoe Stores, Sports Wear
Average Price: Expensive
Area: Saint-Michel/Odéon, 5ème
Address: 49 Boulevard Saint-Michel
75005 Paris France
Phone: 01 56 81 31 32

#335
ZARA
Category: Women's Clothing, Men's Clothing
Average Price: Modest
Area: Beaubourg, 4ème
Address: 88 Rue Rivoli
75004 Paris France
Phone: 01 44 54 20 42

#336
Chanel Boutique
Category: Jewelry
Average Price: Exclusive
Area: Place Vendôme, 1er
Address: 18 Place Vendôme
75001 Paris France
Phone: 01 40 98 55 55

#337
Pretty Box
Category: Used, Vintage & Consignment
Average Price: Modest
Area: Marais Nord, 3ème, Marais
Address: 46 Rue De Saintonge
75003 Paris France
Phone: 01 48 04 81 71

#338
La Tuile À Loup
Category: Arts & Crafts, Tableware
Average Price: Expensive
Area: 5ème, Port Royal/Gobelins
Address: 35 Rue Daubenton
75005 Paris France
Phone: 01 47 07 28 90

#339
Kookaï
Category: Women's Clothing
Average Price: Expensive
Area: Marais, 4ème
Address: 8 Rue Rosiers
75004 Paris France
Phone: 01 42 72 54 71

#340
L'Interloque
Category: Thrift Stores
Average Price: Modest
Area: Mairie Du 18e/Lamarck, 18ème
Address: 7 Rue Trétaigne
75018 Paris France
Phone: 01 46 06 08 86

#341
Les Ateliers
Category: Fashion, Coffee & Tea, Bars
Average Price: Modest
Area: Etienne Marcel/Montorgueil
Address: 6 Rue De Cléry
75002 Paris France
Phone: 01 40 13 00 16

#342
The Collection
Category: Home Decor
Average Price: Expensive
Area: Marais Nord, 3ème, Marais
Address: 33 Rue Poitou
75003 Paris France
Phone: 01 42 77 04 20

#343
Morgan
Category: Women's Clothing
Average Price: Modest
Area: Champs-Elysées, 8ème
Address: 92 Ave Des Champs-Elysées
75008 Paris France
Phone: 01 58 56 21 49

#344
K-Way
Category: Men's Clothing, Women's Clothing
Average Price: Modest
Area: Ledru-Rollin, 11ème
Address: 35 Rue De Charonne
75011 Paris France
Phone: 01 47 00 04 92

#345
Heaven
Category: Women's Clothing
Average Price: Modest
Area: 4ème, Marais
Address: 16 Rue Pont Louis -Philippe
75004 Paris France
Phone: 01 42 77 38 89

#346
Wait Paris
Category: Concept Shops
Average Price: Modest
Area: République, Arts & Métiers
Address: 9 Rue Notre Dame De Nazareth
75003 Paris France
Phone: 09 82 52 84 34

#347
L'êtreange
Category: Concept Shops, Home Decor
Average Price: Modest
Area: Marais, 4ème
Address: 8 Rue d'Ormesson
75004 Paris France
Phone: 01 44 61 56 40

#348
DKS
Category: Women's Clothing, Men's Clothing
Average Price: Modest
Area: Beaubourg, 3ème, Arts &
Métiers/Rambuteau
Address: 44 Rue Beaubourg
75003 Paris France
Phone: 01 48 87 63 64

#349
Culotte
Category: Accessories, Jewelry
Average Price: Modest
Area: Colonel Fabien/Goncourt, 10ème
Address: 25 Rue Sambre Et Meuse
75011 Paris France
Phone: 06 03 43 73 77

#350
Sauver Le Monde Des Hommes
Category: Men's Clothing, Accessories
Average Price: Expensive
Area: République, Canal St Martin
Address: 8 Rue Beaurepaire
75010 Paris France
Phone: 09 84 83 82 28

#351
H&M
Category: Men's Clothing, Women's Clothing,
Children's Clothing
Average Price: Inexpensive
Area: Saint-Lazare/Grands Magasins, 9ème
Address: 54 Bd Haussmann
75009 Paris France
Phone: 01 55 31 92 50

#352
French Touche
Category: Jewelry, Arts & Crafts, Fashion
Average Price: Modest
Area: Batignolles, 17ème
Address: 90 Rue Legendre
75017 Paris France
Phone: 01 42 63 31 36

#353
Nag Champa
Category: Women's Clothing
Average Price: Expensive
Area: Beaubourg, 3ème
Address: 158 Rue Saint Martin
75003 Paris France
Phone: 01 48 04 07 54

#354
Uniqlo
Category: Women's Clothing, Men's Clothing,
Children's Clothing
Average Price: Modest
Area: Saint-Lazare/Grands Magasins, 9ème
Address: 17 Rue Scribe
75009 Paris France
Phone: 01 58 18 30 55

#355
Freep'star
Category: Used, Vintage & Consignment
Average Price: Modest
Area: Marais, 4ème
Address: 20 Rue De Rivoli
75004 Paris France
Phone: 01 42 77 63 43

#356
Look
Category: Used, Vintage & Consignment,
Accessories, Women's Clothing
Average Price: Modest
Area: Pigalle, 9ème
Address: 50 Rue Condorcet
75009 Paris France
Phone: 01 40 16 93 30

#357
Bubble Wood
Category: Men's Clothing, Women's Clothing
Average Price: Modest
Area: Marais, 3ème
Address: 4 Rue Elzévir
75003 Paris France
Phone: 09 66 43 05 61

#358
Charvet
Category: Accessories, Men's Clothing,
Sewing & Alterations
Average Price: Exclusive
Area: Place Vendôme, 1er
Address: 28 Place Vendôme
75001 Paris France
Phone: 01 42 60 30 70

#359
Boutique Emmaüs Charonne
Category: Used, Vintage & Consignment
Average Price: Inexpensive
Area: Ledru-Rollin, 11ème
Address: 54 Rue Charonne
75011 Paris France
Phone: 01 48 07 02 28

#360
American Vintage
Category: Women's Clothing
Average Price: Modest
Area: Marais, 3ème
Address: 10 Rue Des Francs-Bourgeois
75003 Paris France
Phone: 01 42 77 98 73

#361
Aoshida
Category: Women's Clothing
Average Price: Expensive
Area: Tour Eiffel/Champ De Mars, 7ème
Address: 117 Rue St Dominique
75007 Paris France
Phone: 09 67 21 15 10

#362
Deca Belle
Category: Men's Clothing, Women's Clothing
Average Price: Modest
Area: Bastille, 11ème
Address: 8 Rue De Charonne
75011 Paris France
Phone: 01 47 00 05 62

#363
Guerrisol
Category: Used, Vintage & Consignment
Average Price: Inexpensive
Area: Guy Moquet/Saint Ouen, 17ème
Address: 67 Avenue De Clichy
75017 Paris France
Phone: 01 44 70 04 36

#364
Lnj
Category: Fashion
Average Price: Inexpensive
Area: Grands Boulevards/Sentier, 2ème
Address: 15 Boulevard Poissonnière
75009 Paris France
Phone: 01 42 33 52 22

#365
COS
Category: Women's Clothing, Men's Clothing
Average Price: Modest
Area: Bastille, 11ème
Address: 18 Rue De Charonne
75011 Paris France
Phone: 01 70 08 84 50

#366
Kim Thanh
Category: Gift Shops
Average Price: Modest
Area: Place d'Italie, 13ème
Address: 69 Avenue Ivry
75013 Paris France
Phone: 01 45 83 62 00

#367
Promod
Category: Women's Clothing
Average Price: Modest
Area: Opéra, 9ème
Address: 6 Boulevard Des Capucines
75009 Paris France
Phone: 01 40 07 02 74

#368
Gucci
Category: Shoe Stores, Watches, Accessories
Average Price: Exclusive
Area: Avenue Montaigne
Address: 60 Avenue Montaigne
75008 Paris France
Phone: 01 56 69 80 80

#369
Le Rocketship
Category: Home Decor, Concept Shops
Average Price: Modest
Area: Pigalle, 9ème
Address: 13 Bis Rue Henry Monnier
75009 Paris France
Phone: 01 48 78 23 66

#370
Les Ateliers Ruby
Category: Accessories
Average Price: Exclusive
Area: Bourse, 1er
Address: 1 Rue Hérold
75001 Paris France
Phone: 01 40 28 93 07

#371
Asphodèle
Category: Used, Vintage & Consignment
Average Price: Expensive
Area: Richelieu-Drouot, 9ème
Address: 44 Rue Du Faubourg Montmartre
75009 Paris France
Phone: 01 42 46 91 88

#372
Balmain
Category: Fashion
Average Price: Exclusive
Area: Champs-Elysées, 8ème
Address: 44 Rue François 1er
75008 Paris France
Phone: 01 47 20 35 34

#373
Caprices
Category: Women's Clothing, Men's Clothing
Average Price: Modest
Area: 14ème
Address: 130 Ave Du Général
Leclerc 75014 Paris France
Phone: 01 40 44 46 01

#374
Come On Eileen
Category: Used, Vintage &
Consignment, Accessories
Average Price: Modest
Area: Ledru-Rollin, 11ème
Address: 16 Rue Taillandiers
75011 Paris France
Phone: 01 43 38 12 11

#375
La Jolie Garde Robe
Category: Used, Vintage & Consignment
Average Price: Expensive
Area: Marais Nord, 3ème
Address: 15 Rue Commines
75003 Paris France
Phone: 01 42 72 13 90

#376
Franprix
Category: Department Stores
Average Price: Modest
Area: 2ème, Bourse
Address: 11 Rue Mail
75002 Paris France
Phone: 01 42 60 12 43

#377
Tally Weilj
Category: Women's Clothing
Average Price: Inexpensive
Area: 1er, Palais Royal/Musée Du Louvre
Address: Forum Des Halles Niveau -3
75001 Paris France
Phone: 06 15 68 60 00

#378
Flamant
Category: Home Decor, Furniture Stores
Average Price: Expensive
Area: Saint-Germain-Des-Prés, 6ème
Address: 8 Rue Abbaye
75006 Paris France
Phone: 01 56 81 12 40

#379
Célio
Category: Fashion
Average Price: Modest
Area: Bastille, 12ème
Address: 26 Faubourg Saint Antoine
75012 Paris France
Phone: 01 43 42 31 68

#380
Azag
Category: Home Decor, Accessories,
Concept Shops
Average Price: Modest
Area: 4ème, Marais
Address: 9 Rue François Miron
75004 Paris France
Phone: 01 48 04 08 18

#381
Monop Maine
Category: Department Stores
Average Price: Modest
Area: 14ème, Denfert-Rochereau
Address: 151 Ave Du Maine
75014 Paris France
Phone: 01 40 43 19 10

#382
Monop
Category: Department Stores
Average Price: Modest
Area: 3ème, Marais Nord, Arts &
Métiers/Rambuteau, Marais
Address: 5 Rue Des Haudriettes
75003 Paris France
Phone: 01 42 76 09 11

#383
L'Appartement
Category: Personal Shopping
Average Price: Modest
Area: Musée d'Orsay, 7ème
Address: 16 Rue De Bellechasse
75007 Paris France
Phone: 01 45 51 88 88

#384
La Chapellerie Julias
Category: Men's Clothing, Women's Clothing
Average Price: Modest
Area: 18ème, Barbès/Goutte d'Or
Address: 59 Bd Barbès
75018 Paris France
Phone: 01 42 64 16 33

#385
American Vintage
Category: Women's Clothing, Accessories
Average Price: Expensive
Area: Etienne Marcel/Montorgueil, 2ème
Address: 62 Rue Tiquetonne
75002 Paris France
Phone: 01 42 21 46 73

#386
Via Veneto
Category: Men's Clothing, Women's Clothing
Average Price: Expensive
Area: 14ème
Address: 72 Rue d'Alésia
75014 Paris France
Phone: 01 45 45 66 49

#387
La Piscine
Category: Men's Clothing, Women's Clothing
Average Price: Modest
Area: Marais, 4ème
Address: 13 Rue Des Francs-Bourgeois
75004 Paris France
Phone: 01 48 87 59 24

#388
Idéco
Category: Home Decor, Jewelry
Average Price: Modest
Area: Belleville/Ménilmontant, 19ème
Address: 19 Rue Beaurepaire
75010 Paris France
Phone: 01 42 01 00 11

#389
Zen Ethic
Category: Jewelry, Accessories
Average Price: Modest
Area: Marais, 3ème, Marais Nord
Address: 52 Rue Des Francs Bourgeois
75019 Paris France
Phone: 01 53 19 94 85

#390
Monoprix
Category: Grocery
Average Price: Modest
Area: Europe/Miromesnil, 8ème
Address: 30 Rue d'Astorg
75008 Paris France
Phone: 01 40 98 00 30

#391
Tara Jarmon
Category: Fashion
Average Price: Modest
Area: Auteuil, 16ème
Address: 51 Rue Passy
75016 Paris France
Phone: 01 45 24 65 20

#392
Petit Bateau
Category: Women's Clothing,
Children's Clothing
Average Price: Modest
Area: 6ème
Address: 53 Bis Rue De Sèvres
75006 Paris France
Phone: 01 45 49 48 38

#393
Stock Etam
Category: Women's Clothing, Lingerie
Average Price: Inexpensive
Area: Montmartre, 18ème
Address: 2 Rue De Clignarcourt
75018 Paris France
Phone: 01 46 06 09 49

#394
Les Petites...
Category: Women's Clothing
Average Price: Modest
Area: Bourse, 1er
Address: 5 Place Des Victoires
75001 Paris France
Phone: 09 65 30 87 86

#395
Art Du Basic
Category: Women's Clothing
Average Price: Modest
Area: Marais, 3ème, Marais Nord
Address: 78 Rue Vieille Du Temple
75004 Paris France
Phone: 01 44 54 95 14

#396
La Petite Boutique
Category: Jewelry
Average Price: Modest
Area: République, 3ème
Address: 18 Rue Meslay
75003 Paris France
Phone: 09 50 51 32 48

#397
Shakespeare And Company
Category: Bookstores
Average Price: Modest
Area: Notre Dame De Paris
Address: 37 Rue De La Bûcherie
75005 Paris France
Phone: 01 43 25 40 93

#398
Chercheminippes
Category: Used, Vintage & Consignment
Average Price: Inexpensive
Area: 6ème, Montparnasse
Address: 102 Rue Cherche Midi
75006 Paris France
Phone: 01 45 44 97 96

#399
Massaï-Mara Créations
Category: Accessories, Children's Clothing
Average Price: Modest
Area: Nation/Vincennes, 11ème
Address: 40 Rue Chanzy
75011 Paris France
Phone: 01 43 73 06 60

#400
Maison Ivre
Category: Home Decor, Tableware
Average Price: Expensive
Area: Saint-Germain-Des-Prés, 6ème
Address: 38 Rue Jacob
75006 Paris France
Phone: 01 42 60 01 85

#401
Loft Design By
Category: Women's Clothing, Men's Clothing
Average Price: Modest
Area: Champs-Elysées, 17ème
Address: 22 Avenue De La Grande Armée
75017 Paris France
Phone: 01 45 72 13 53

#402
Lin Et Petits Points
Category: Cards & Stationery,
Bookstores, Men's Clothing
Average Price: Modest
Area: 15ème
Address: 119 Avenue Félix Faure
75015 Paris France
Phone: 01 45 54 78 29

#403
La Boîte À Joujoux
Category: Toy Stores
Average Price: Modest
Area: Richelieu-Drouot, 9ème
Address: 41-43 Passage Jouffroy
75009 Paris France
Phone: 01 48 24 58 37

#404
No Smoking
Category: Women's Clothing
Average Price: Modest
Area: Pigalle, 9ème
Address: 57 Rue Condorcet
75009 Paris France
Phone: 01 48 78 48 72

#405
Anne Throude
Category: Women's Clothing
Average Price: Modest
Area: Pigalle, Montmartre, 18ème
Address: 7 Rue Houdon
75018 Paris France
Phone: 01 42 51 35 58

#406
Etam Prêt À Porter
Category: Women's Clothing
Average Price: Modest
Area: Saint-Michel/Odéon, 5ème
Address: 9 Boulevard St Michel
75005 Paris France
Phone: 01 43 54 79 20

#407
Exquisautoir
Category: Jewelry, Accessories
Average Price: Modest
Area: Tour Eiffel/Champ De Mars, 15ème
Address: 59 Ave De Motte Picquet
75015 Paris France
Phone: 09 81 86 09 70

#408
Emmaüs Alternatives
Category: Used, Vintage &
Consignment, Thrift Stores
Average Price: Inexpensive
Area: Beaubourg, 4ème
Address: 35 Rue Quincampoix
75004 Paris France
Phone: 01 44 61 69 19

#409
Apr-77
Category: Men's Clothing, Women's Clothing
Average Price: Expensive
Area: Bastille, 11ème
Address: 7 Rue Charonne
75011 Paris France
Phone: 01 43 38 39 74

#410
Wasted
Category: Accessories, Men's Clothing,
Women's Clothing
Average Price: Modest
Area: Châtelet/Les Halles, 1er
Address: 66 Rue Saint-Denis
75001 Paris France
Phone: 01 73 75 37 81

#411
Monoprix
Category: Department Stores
Average Price: Modest
Area: 14ème
Address: 129 Rue Alésia
75014 Paris France
Phone: 01 40 44 41 78

#412
Hermès
Category: Leather Goods
Average Price: Exclusive
Area: Champs-Elysées, 8ème
Address: 42 Avenue George V
75008 Paris France
Phone: 01 47 20 48 51

#413
Altermundi
Category: Fashion,
Home Decor
Average Price: Modest
Area: Ledru-Rollin, 11ème
Address: 39 Rue De Charonne
75011 Paris France
Phone: 01 48 05 11 81

#414
L'International Records
Category: Vinyl Records
Average Price: Modest
Area: Oberkampf/Parmentier, 11ème
Address: 12 Rue Moret
75011 Paris France
Phone: 09 80 57 12 61

#415
Mellow Yellow
Category: Shoe Stores
Average Price: Modest
Area: Marais, 4ème, Marais Nord
Address: 43 Rue Des Francs Bourgeois
75004 Paris France
Phone: 01 44 54 11 51

#416
Le Jupon Rouge
Category: Furniture Stores, Thrift Stores,
Used, Vintage & Consignment, Hobby Shops
Average Price: Modest
Area: Strasbourg-St Denis
Address: 12 Rue Mayran
75009 Paris France
Phone: 01 48 78 54 54

#417
ZARA
Category: Women's Clothing
Average Price: Modest
Area: Montparnasse, 15ème
Address: 33 Avenue Du Maine
75015 Paris France
Phone: 01 40 64 04 40

#418
O-Paris
Category: Women's Clothing,
Men's Clothing, Accessories
Average Price: Modest
Area: Marais, 4ème
Address: 16 Rue Du Bourg Tibourg
75004 Paris France
Phone: 01 42 76 00 44

#419
Size-Factory
Category: Plus Size Fashion
Average Price: Modest
Area: 13ème
Address: 15 Rue Marie-Andrée Lagroua
Weill-Hallé 75013 Paris France
Phone: 09 73 14 54 08

#420
Monoprix Mozart
Category: Department Stores
Average Price: Modest
Area: Auteuil, 16ème
Address: 49 Rue d'Auteuil
75016 Paris France
Phone: 01 45 24 30 53

#421
Allsaints
Category: Women's Clothing, Men's Clothing
Average Price: Expensive
Area: Marais, 4ème
Address: 23 Rue Des Rosiers
75004 Paris France
Phone: 01 84 88 42 37

#422
Gab & Jo
Category: Concept Shops
Average Price: Modest
Area: Saint-Germain-Des-Prés, 6ème
Address: 28 Rue Jacob
75006 Paris France
Phone: 09 84 53 58 43

#423
Richard Fahl
Category: Women's Clothing,
Shoe Stores, Accessories
Average Price: Modest
Area: Châtelet/Les Halles, 1er
Address: 133 Rue Saint-Denis
75001 Paris France
Phone: 01 42 33 53 90

#424
Naf Naf
Category: Women's Clothing,
Leather Goods, Accessories
Average Price: Modest
Area: Champs-Elysées, 17ème
Address: 2 Rue Poncelet
75017 Paris France
Phone: 01 42 67 30 30

#425
C&A
Category: Men's Clothing, Women's Clothing
Average Price: Modest
Area: 4ème, Marais
Address: 2 Le Parvis De
La Défense 92800 Paris France
Phone: 01 47 73 00 12

#426
Antik Batik
Category: Women's Clothing
Average Price: Modest
Area: Saint-Germain-Des-Prés, 6ème
Address: 26 Rue Saint-Sulpice
75006 Paris France
Phone: 01 44 07 68 53

#427
Fripes Therapy
Category: Used, Vintage & Consignment
Average Price: Modest
Area: Marais Nord, 3ème, Marais
Address: 5 Bis Rue Froissart
75003 Paris France
Phone: 01 42 76 02 00

#428
Nomad's Land
Category: Women's Clothing,
Children's Clothing
Average Price: Modest
Area: Oberkampf/Parmentier, 11ème
Address: 20 Rue Oberkampf
75011 Paris France
Phone: 01 48 05 59 45

#429
Boutique BDA
Category: Women's Clothing,
Used, Vintage & Consignment
Average Price: Modest
Area: Batignolles, 17ème
Address: 46 Rue De La Condamine
75017 Paris France
Phone: 01 42 93 54 70

#430
Coup 2 Coeur
Category: Shoe Stores
Average Price: Modest
Area: Saint-Germain-Des-Prés, 6ème
Address: 4 Rue Clement
75006 Paris France
Phone: 01 46 34 00 32

#431
L'espionne
Category: Women's Clothing, Men's Clothing
Average Price: Modest
Area: 17ème
Address: 2 Place Porte Maillot
75017 Paris France
Phone: 01 40 68 23 31

#432
El Ganso
Category: Men's Clothing
Average Price: Modest
Area: Châtelet/Les Halles, 1er
Address: 11 Rue Montmartre
75001 Paris France
Phone: 01 44 82 54 38

#433
Tim Bargeot
Category: Fashion
Average Price: Modest
Area: Châtelet/Les Halles, 1er
Address: 3 Rue De Turbigo
75001 Paris France
Phone: 01 42 21 09 69

#434
Simone
Category: Fashion
Average Price: Modest
Area: Musée d'Orsay, 7ème
Address: 1 Rue De Saint Simon
75007 Paris France
Phone: 01 42 22 81 40

#435
Vanessa Bruno
Category: Women's Clothing
Average Price: Expensive
Area: Marais Nord, 3ème, Marais
Address: 100 Rue Vieille Du Temple
75003 Paris France
Phone: 01 42 77 19 41

#436
Carling
Category: Women's Clothing
Average Price: Modest
Area: 14ème, Denfert-Rochereau
Address: 102 Rue d'Alésia
75014 Paris France
Phone: 01 45 42 43 03

#437
Monoprix
Category: Department Stores
Average Price: Modest
Area: Concorde/Madeleine, 9ème
Address: 9 Boulevard De La Madeleine
75001 Paris France
Phone: 01 42 86 61 54

#438
Size?
Category: Accessories, Shoe Stores,
Children's Clothing
Average Price: Modest
Area: Châtelet/Les Halles, 1er
Address: 16-18 Rue Berger
75001 Paris France
Phone: 01 40 39 02 86

#439
Isakin
Category: Shoe Stores,
Men's Clothing, Accessories
Average Price: Modest
Area: Montmartre, 18ème
Address: 9 Rue André Del Sarte
75018 Paris France
Phone: 09 51 89 41 88

#440
Gerard Darel
Category: Women's Clothing,
Leather Goods, Accessories
Average Price: Modest
Area: Saint-Germain-Des-Prés, 6ème
Address: 174 Bd Saint Germain
75006 Paris France
Phone: 01 45 48 54 80

#441
Marché U
Category: Department Stores, Grocery
Average Price: Modest
Area: Etienne Marcel/Montorgueil, 2ème
Address: 67 Rue Montorgueil
75002 Paris France
Phone: 01 42 36 52 59

#442
Bérénice
Category: Fashion
Average Price: Modest
Area: Marais, 3ème, Marais Nord
Address: 52 Rue Francs Bourgeois
75003 Paris France
Phone: 01 44 59 39 74

#443
René Caovilla
Category: Shoe Stores, Accessories
Average Price: Exclusive
Area: Concorde/Madeleine, 8ème
Address: 23 Fbg St Honoré
75008 Paris France
Phone: 01 42 68 19 55

#444
Bathroom Graffiti
Category: Home Decor, Kitchen & Bath
Average Price: Modest
Area: 16ème
Address: 98 Rue De Longchamp
75016 Paris France
Phone: 01 47 04 32 44

#445
L'Antisèche
Category: Men's Clothing, Women's Clothing
Average Price: Modest
Area: Sorbonne/Panthéon, 5ème
Address: 2 Rue Des Fossés-Saint-Jacques
75005 Paris France
Phone: 01 40 51 85 69

#446
No Good Store
Category: Women's Clothing, Men's Clothing,
Used, Vintage & Consignment
Average Price: Expensive
Area: Pigalle, 9ème
Address: 52 Rue De Martyrs
75009 Paris France
Phone: 01 45 96 00 87

#447
Ligne Claire
Category: Home Decor
Average Price: Inexpensive
Area: Vaugirard/Grenelle, 15ème
Address: 6 Boulevard Garibaldi
75015 Paris France
Phone: 01 42 73 03 09

#448
Louvre Antiq'Bijoux
Category: Jewelry, Antiques, Arts &
Entertainment
Average Price: Modest
Area: Châtelet/Les Halles, 1er
Address: 2 Palais Royal
75001 Paris France
Phone: 01 42 60 64 28

#449
Boutique Renoma
Category: Men's Clothing,
Art Galleries, Accessories
Average Price: Modest
Area: Victor Hugo, Trocadéro/Iéna, 16ème
Address: 129 Bis Rue De La Pompe
75116 Paris France
Phone: 01 44 05 38 26

#450
Estelle Ramousse Modiste
Category: Arts & Crafts, Accessories
Average Price: Modest
Area: Belleville/Ménilmontant, 20ème
Address: 64 Rue De La Mare
75020 Paris France
Phone: 01 77 11 29 04

#451
Aimecube
Category: Men's Clothing,
Women's Clothing, Art Galleries
Average Price: Modest
Area: Châtelet/Les Halles, 1er
Address: 7 Rue Vauvilliers
75001 Paris France
Phone: 01 40 26 55 83

#452
Bocoray
Category: Framing,
Home Decor, Fabric Stores
Average Price: Modest
Area: 9ème, Richelieu-Drouot
Address: 72 Rue Fbg Montmartre
75009 Paris France
Phone: 01 48 78 88 88

#453
Chez Violette
Category: Jewelry, Toy Stores, Home Decor
Average Price: Expensive
Area: Vaugirard/Grenelle, 15ème
Address: 29 Rue Lecourbe
75015 Paris France
Phone: 01 40 61 02 43

#454
Shoeping
Category: Shoe Stores, Women's Clothing
Average Price: Modest
Area: Montmartre, 18ème
Address: 58 Boulevard Rochechouart
75018 Paris France
Phone: 01 42 54 10 15

#455
Kering
Category: Men's Clothing, Women's Clothing
Average Price: Modest
Area: 7ème
Address: 40 Rue De Sèvres
75007 Paris France
Phone: 01 45 64 61 00

#456
La Chaise Longue
Category: Home Decor, Furniture Stores
Average Price: Modest
Area: Montmartre, 18ème
Address: 91 Rue Martyrs
75018 Paris France
Phone: 01 42 62 34 28

#457
The Kooples
Category: Men's Clothing, Women's Clothing
Average Price: Expensive
Area: Palais Royal/Musée Du Louvre, 1er
Address: 191 Rue St Honoré
75001 Paris France
Phone: 01 49 26 05 35

#458
Kookaï Le Stock
Category: Women's Clothing
Average Price: Modest
Area: Arts & Métiers/Rambuteau, 2ème
Address: 82 Rue Réaumur
75002 Paris France
Phone: 01 45 08 93 69

#459
Mirène
Category: Men's Clothing
Average Price: Modest
Area: Châtelet/Les Halles, 4ème
Address: 76 Rue Rivoli
75004 Paris France
Phone: 01 48 87 75 15

#460
Sauver Le Monde Des Hommes
Category: Men's Clothing, Accessories
Average Price: Modest
Area: Montmartre, Pigalle, 18ème
Address: 1 Rue Des Trois Frères
75018 Paris France
Phone: 09 73 26 16 78

#461
Ulla Popken
Category: Men's Clothing,
Women's Clothing, Lingerie
Average Price: Expensive
Area: Chaussée d'Antin, 9ème
Address: 32 Bd Haussmann
75009 Paris France
Phone: 01 53 24 68 10

#462
Zadig Et Voltaire
Category: Women's Clothing
Average Price: Exclusive
Area: Place Vendôme, 1er
Address: 9 Rue 29 Juillet
75001 Paris France
Phone: 01 42 92 00 80

#463
Calzedonia
Category: Women's Clothing
Average Price: Modest
Area: Vaugirard/Grenelle, 15ème
Address: 34 Rue Du Commerce
75015 Paris France
Phone: 09 67 34 87 51

#464
Chapeaux Marguerite
Category: Accessories
Average Price: Modest
Area: Bercy, 12ème
Address: 14 Ave De Corbéra
75012 Paris France
Phone: 01 43 41 10 23

#465
Maison Fabre
Category: Arts & Crafts, Accessories
Average Price: Expensive
Area: Palais Royal/Musée Du Louvre, 1er
Address: 128 Galerie De Valois
75001 Paris France
Phone: 01 42 60 75 88

#466
Ysasu
Category: Shoe Stores
Average Price: Expensive
Area: Montmartre, 18ème
Address: 19 Rue André Del Sarte
75018 Paris France
Phone: 01 42 52 10 44

#467
Klin d'Œil
Category: Men's Clothing,
Women's Clothing
Average Price: Modest
Area: Oberkampf/Parmentier
Address: 6 Rue Deguerry
75011 Paris France
Phone: 01 77 15 22 30

#468
Chapeau Fleurelle
Category: Accessories
Average Price: Modest
Area: Châtelet/Les Halles, 1er
Address: 91 Rue Saint Honoré
75001 Paris France
Phone: 01 40 26 23 72

#469
Coton Doux
Category: Men's Clothing, Women's Clothing
Average Price: Inexpensive
Area: Saint-Lazare/Grands Magasins, 9ème
Address: 82 Rue St Lazare
75009 Paris France
Phone: 01 44 63 03 83

#470
Monoprix
Category: Grocery, Department Stores
Average Price: Modest
Area: Belleville/Ménilmontant, 19ème
Address: 133 Rue De Belleville
75019 Paris France
Phone: 01 42 39 95 37

#471
Antoine Et Lili
Category: Women's Clothing, Home Decor
Average Price: Modest
Area: Montmartre, 18ème
Address: 90 Rue Des Martyrs
75018 Paris France
Phone: 01 42 58 10 22

#472
Maison Scotch
Category: Accessories, Women's Clothing
Average Price: Expensive
Area: Marais, 4ème
Address: 42 Rue Vieille Du Temple
75004 Paris France
Phone: 01 42 71 02 67

#473
Oliver Jung
Category: Women's Clothing
Average Price: Modest
Area: Châtelet/Les Halles, Palais
Royal/Musée Du Louvre, 1er
Address: 3 Rue Louvre
75001 Paris France
Phone: 01 42 61 53 23

#474
Nose
Category: Perfume, Cosmetics & Beauty
Supply, Personal Shopping
Average Price: Expensive
Area: Etienne Marcel/Montorgueil, 2ème
Address: 20 Rue Bachaumont
75002 Paris France
Phone: 01 40 26 46 03

#475
Comme Des Garçons Pocket
Category: Men's Clothing
Average Price: Modest
Area: Marais Nord, 3ème, Marais
Address: 31 Rue Debelleyme
75003 Paris France
Phone: 01 42 72 15 12

#476
Petit Bateau
Category: Children's Clothing, Women's
Clothing, Lingerie
Average Price: Modest
Area: Concorde/Madeleine, 8ème
Address: 13 Rue Tronchet
75008 Paris France
Phone: 01 42 65 26 26

#477
Maje
Category: Women's Clothing
Average Price: Modest
Area: Nation/Vincennes, 11ème
Address: 6 Rue Immeubles Industriels
75011 Paris France
Phone: 01 43 70 26 56

#478
By Luna
Category: Women's Clothing
Average Price: Modest
Area: Marais, Bastille, 4ème
Address: 68 Rue Saint Antoine
75004 Paris France
Phone: 01 42 74 09 31

#479
Rose Bunker
Category: Concept Shops, Gift Shops
Average Price: Modest
Area: Montmartre, 18ème
Address: 10 Rue Aristide Bruant
75018 Paris France
Phone: 01 42 57 90 62

#480
Darkland
Category: Women's Clothing, Accessories,
Men's Clothing
Average Price: Expensive
Area: Châtelet/Les Halles, 1er
Address: 3 Rue Sauval
75001 Paris 01 France
Phone: 01 42 36 61 02

#481
Jezabel
Category: Shoe Stores
Average Price: Inexpensive
Area: 7ème, Tour Eiffel/Champ De Mars
Address: 49 Rue Cler
75007 Paris France
Phone: 01 45 56 06 86

#482
Comptoir Du Désert
Category: Women's Clothing
Average Price: Expensive
Area: Ledru-Rollin, 11ème
Address: 74 Rue De La Roquette
75011 Paris France
Phone: 01 40 21 01 71

#483
Divine
Category: Accessories
Average Price: Modest
Area: Concorde/Madeleine, 9ème
Address: 3 Rue Scribe
75009 Paris France
Phone: 01 40 06 03 14

#484
Sommier
Category: Costumes, Bridal,
Children's Clothing
Average Price: Modest
Area: Strasbourg-St Denis
Address: 4 Passage Brady
75010 Paris France
Phone: 09 50 79 58 11

#485
Diwali
Category: Accessories, Jewelry
Average Price: Modest
Area: 5ème, Sorbonne/Panthéon
Address: 47-49 Rue Mouffetard
75005 Paris France
Phone: 01 43 36 19 02

#486
Du Jour Au Lendemain
Category: Women's Clothing
Average Price: Modest
Area: Ledru-Rollin, 11ème
Address: 85 Rue De La Roquette
75011 Paris France
Phone: 01 43 73 81 16

#487
Le 18
Category: Home Decor, Fashion
Average Price: Modest
Area: Ledru-Rollin, 11ème
Address: 18 Rue Keller
75011 Paris France
Phone: 01 48 05 55 62

#488
Consuelo Zoelly
Category: Women's Clothing, Men's Clothing
Average Price: Expensive
Area: Marais, 3ème, Marais Nord
Address: 22 Rue Perle
75003 Paris France
Phone: 01 42 72 09 16

#489
Le Labo
Category: Gift Shops
Average Price: Modest
Area: Etienne Marcel/Montorgueil, 2ème
Address: 4 Passage Grand Cerf
75002 Paris France
Phone: 01 40 13 01 58

#490
Kookaï
Category: Women's Clothing
Average Price: Expensive
Area: Marais, Bastille, 4ème
Address: 70 Rue Saint Antoine
75004 Paris France
Phone: 01 40 29 91 63

#491
H&M
Category: Men's Clothing, Women's Clothing,
Children's Clothing
Average Price: Modest
Area: Beaubourg, 4ème
Address: 88 Rue De Rivoli
75001 Paris France
Phone: 01 53 01 87 40

#492
Cache Cache
Category: Women's Clothing
Average Price: Modest
Area: Vaugirard/Grenelle, 15ème
Address: 63 Rue Lecourbe
75015 Paris France
Phone: 01 43 06 49 92

#493
Les Beaux Mecs
Category: Used, Vintage & Consignment
Average Price: Inexpensive
Area: Ledru-Rollin, 11ème
Address: 18 Rue Jules Vallès
75011 Paris France
Phone: 09 82 50 93 35

#494
IKKS General Store
Category: Men's Clothing, Women's Clothing
Average Price: Modest
Area: 2ème, Etienne Marcel/Montorgueil
Address: 3 Rue d'Argout
75002 Paris France
Phone: 01 40 28 18 38

#495
Nunettes
Category: Eyewear & Opticians
Average Price: Modest
Area: Barbès/Goutte d'Or, 18ème
Address: 5/7 Rue Ordener
75018 Paris France
Phone: 01 53 26 75 61

#496
Idéco Store
Category: Home Decor,
Gift Shops, Kitchen & Bath
Average Price: Modest
Area: 15ème, Vaugirard/Grenelle
Address: 94 Rue Du Commerce
75015 Paris France
Phone: 01 77 17 76 37

#497
Robert Le Héros
Category: Accessories
Average Price: Modest
Area: Saint-Germain-Des-Prés, 6ème
Address: 13 Rue Quatre Vents
75006 Paris France
Phone: 01 43 54 99 14

#498
Eiffel Depot Vente E.D.V
Category: Accessories, Women's Clothing
Average Price: Modest
Area: Tour Eiffel/Champ De Mars, 15ème
Address: 53 Ave La Motte Picquet
75015 Paris France
Phone: 01 42 73 53 26

#499
Barbara Ines
Category: Fashion
Average Price: Modest
Area: 16ème, Auteuil
Address: 38 Rue Doct Blanche
75016 Paris France
Phone: 06 28 53 29 42

#500
Eliz
Category: Women's Clothing, Sewing &
Alterations, Men's Clothing
Average Price: Modest
Area: 20ème, Nation/Vincennes
Address: 76 Rue Saint-Blaise
75020 Paris France
Phone: 01 43 56 87 07

Made in the USA
San Bernardino, CA
02 November 2019

59356764R00029